INFORMATION, MANAGEMENT AND PARTICIPATION

A new approach from public health in Brazil

FRANCESCO NOTARBARTOLO DI VILLAROSA

FRANK CASS
LONDON • PORTLAND, OR

Published in 1998 in Great Britain by
FRANK CASS PUBLISHERS
Newbury House, 900 Eastern Avenue,
London IG2 7HH England

and in the United States of America by
FRANK CASS PUBLISHERS
c/o ISBS, 5804 N.E. Hassalo Street,
Portland, Oregon 97213-3644

Website http://www.frankcass.com

British Library Cataloguing in Publication Data

Di Villarosa, Francesco Notarbartolo
Information management and participation : a new approach from public health in Brazil
1. Medical informatics – Brazil 2. Health services administration – Brazil – Data processing
I. Title
362.1'0981'09049

ISBN 0 7146 4353 X (paper)

Library of Congress Cataloging-in-Publication Data

Notarbartolo di Villarosa, Francesco, 1960–
Information, management, and participation : a new approach from public health in Brazil / Francesco Notarbartolo di Villarosa.
p. cm.
Based on the author's thesis (DPhil – Institute of Development, University of Sussex)
Includes bibliographical references and index.
ISBN 0-7146-4353-X (pbk).
1. Public health – Research – Brazil – Salvador – Methodology.
2. Public health – Brazil – Salvador – Data processing.
3. Public health – Brazil – Salvador – Decision making.
I. Title.
RA440.87.B6N68 1997
362.1'0981 – dc21 97-19271

Printed in Great Britain by
Arrowhead Books Ltd, Reading

To my wife Vera

Contents

List of Tables

List of Figures

List of Maps

Acknowledgements

This book is the product of a DPhil thesis which I wrote at the Institute of Development Studies at the University of Sussex. It is the result also of my participation as a staff member in an Italian technical co-operation project in Brazil. Hence, it has benefited from discussions with a number of people from different countries.

I wish to thank Emanuel de Kadt, who was my supervisor at the IDS: his commitment as a tutor, his comments as a scholar and his encouragement as a friend were all equally important. Thanks also go to Mick Moore of the IDS and Arturo Israel of the World Bank, who examined my thesis and provided helpful comments for its later adjustment and publication as a book.

I wish to thank also my colleagues of the Italian Co-operation project, with whom I had the privilege to work and exchange ideas in the field: Francesco Ripa di Meana, Claudio Grego and especially Renato Tasca. Thanks also to Eugênio Vilaça Mendes of PAHO and Rosa Virgínia Fernandes of the health district of Pau da Lima.

Last but not least, special thanks go to my parents Rodrigo and Anna, who constantly motivated me to transform the practical experience of a project into a book.

Preface

Since the early 1980s, development policy has obsessively addressed the issues of structural adjustment, the reduction of state expenditures and the achievement of financial or macro-economic equilibria. In most poor countries the resources available for social policy lessened dramatically. Social betterment would have to await improvement in the economy, and ministers of finance gave social policy issues little priority.

In the second half of that decade many came to realise that the new policies harmed the poor above all. While this did not bring a fundamental reappraisal, it did result in significant (and novel) efforts to try to ensure that the limited funds available for social programmes would benefit those most in need. Much was written about the idea of *targeting*. Countries tried to adjust social policy management accordingly, often in combination with decentralisation. Yet the results were seldom up to expectations. With very few exceptions, service delivery structures and administrative capacities were simply not up to the challenge. People did not pay enough attention to thinking through and elaborating what was necessary for implementation. Top-down procedures and professional 'technocratic' attitudes, under attack from various emerging new schools of thought, were also blamed for these failures – bottom-up, flexible and participatory approaches were presented as alternatives, even panaceas.

The work which provided the subject for the present study was started in the latter part of this period, in a recently 're-democratised' Brazil. Its 1988 Constitution must contain a wider range of 'fundamental rights' and more equity-related promises – among them a range of formal, universal 'rights to health' – than any other. The problem with such promises is how to begin fulfilling them: what, apart from enabling legislation, is required to make them real for ordinary people? Francesco Notarbartolo di Villarosa and his colleagues were contracted by an Italian Co-operation Agency to help do just that in a poor area of Salvador de Bahia in Brazil. This book tells how they went about the job of helping to transform the management of a poorly functioning health system district, and how they built the tools with which to deliver a more equitable service, one that could function well for the poor. It is a tale well told, combining an accessible discussion of some central questions in the theory of development policy management, with a hands-on description of the actual process that is as fascinating as it is relevant to 'practitioners' in a whole range of people-related activities in developing countries.

Di Villarosa does not become a hostage of the often polarised debates around these issues. It is not just that he gives credit to bottom-up and top-down, to expert-driven and participatory approaches, to precision and to relevance, to 'blueprint' and 'process', and that he does not make Manichaeic lists praising one and damning the other. The point is that he shows precisely when and how elements from the 'opposing traditions' need to be combined for greatest operational impact.

Health-care services need to make decisions based on overview data, ideally providing most resources where need is greatest. Yet they tend to be supply-driven, with norms and tasks ('targets') set by some distant central office. With luck they take account of local conditions by considering the patterns of ill-health seen in clinics. They do not think about what they do not see: the people who do not turn up at the health facility, the environmental hazards not on official maps. They do not have that knowledge. To *build up* knowledge, they need flexible inputs from below: only rapid appraisal methods can provide those at manageable cost. To *use* it, for decision-making and resource allocation, they need clear, no-nonsense rules that leave minimal margin for error or arbitrariness. They also need to be reasonably sure of the reliability and validity of the information used, and that it really identifies where need is greatest and where efforts should be most intense.

Di Villarosa guides us through the steps (and the learning process) taken by a group of Italians and Brazilians in Salvador de Bahia. In relating the journey to existing theories, he makes it relevant beyond the case-study and beyond the health sector. In contrast to those who merely proclaim the excellence of rapid appraisal methods, he actually tries to assess their value in one of the Technical Appendices, by comparing outcomes with those of more conventional (household survey) methodology. Questions remain, but it shows the way and provides significant support for a judicious use of rapid appraisal in a policy management methodology which also needs to worry about precision and specificity. And, rather than merely proclaiming the merits of targeting to make efficient yet equitable use of limited resources, he explains how one can pinpoint – for action – those truly in need, and he demonstrates that geographic information systems are easily usable and effective tools, not esoteric hi-tech playthings.

Many have lamented the lack of effectiveness in development policy implementation. Many others have observed that theoretical insights in the social development field make little difference to what actually gets done. Here is a book that brings theory and practice together to contribute to effective social policy management in less-developed countries. I have learned a great deal from it. I am sure others will, too.

EMANUEL DE KADT
Institute of Development Studies
University of Sussex

Introduction

This book deals with problems of management of people-oriented projects in less developed countries (LDCs). These are the projects which refer to activities or sectors such as institutional development, health, family planning, education, rural development, and so on. A case-study is analysed from a health district project in the urban area of Pau da Lima, Salvador de Bahia, Brazil. A period of approximately three years (mid-1989 to mid-1992) is considered. I was on the project staff as a sociologist. The focus of the analysis is on the aspects of information-handling of this project.[1]

The Theoretical Question and its Relevance for Policy

This study focuses on a theoretical question which is relevant for the implementation of people-oriented projects – the question of the relation between a blueprint and a process approach.

The adoption of a process, flexible approach is usually suggested for managing people-oriented projects. However, the resulting performance is all too often disappointing. Vague goals and targets, never ending bargaining processes, poorly programmed activities, ineffective implementation, and lack of monitoring and evaluation are frequently reported among the problems of projects adopting a process approach. We argue that these projects should integrate an overall process approach with elements from the blueprint approach – although avoiding the rigidities of the latter.

This is not just a purely academic question. Poverty (and people-oriented projects aiming at reducing it) emerged again at the beginning of the present decade as a priority issue on the international agenda. This was basically a consequence of the growing awareness of the social costs of structural adjustment programmes.

The 1980s have been defined as the 'lost decade' for most of the developing world – mainly for Sub-Saharan Africa and Latin America. Figures for the Latin American continent as a whole show an increase in the absolute number of people in poverty during the decade – especially in urban areas.[2] As far as Brazil is concerned, between 1979 and 1986 the percentage of urban poor and urban indigent households increased, respectively, from 30 to 34 per cent, and from ten to 13 per cent.[3]

This situation led several countries to set specific programmes aimed at reducing poverty.[4] These programmes are, nowadays, part of the 'new conventional wisdom',[5] boosted by the main development agencies.[6] The World Bank indicates two basic strategies for reducing poverty: promoting the productive use of the poor's most abundant asset – labour; and providing basic social services (mainly primary health care and education) to the poor.[7] Within a general framework of fiscal discipline, and in order to be really cost-effective, these programmes must be (a) well-targeted towards the most vulnerable groups of the population, and (b) tailor-made according to the specific needs of the latter.

Many programmes are being implemented at this time in Latin America for the reduction of poverty. These programmes are supposed to focus on the most vulnerable groups. However, they frequently run into problems of management and implementation. The case of Brazil is illustrative in this respect.

In 1990 the public expenditure for the social sector as a whole represented almost 19 per cent of the GNP of Brazil.[8] This percentage was similar to that of other countries with a comparable level of economic development. But these resources were allocated with no equity at all. Only 15 per cent of these funds actually reached the poorest 20 per cent of the population. In contrast, 21 per cent of these funds were allocated to the richest 20 per cent of the population.[9] In 1990 Brazilian poor were estimated to be 24 millions (17.4 per cent of the population). If social programmes were effectively targeted towards them, 0.8 per cent of the Brazilian GNP would be sufficient to eliminate absolute poverty in the country.[10]

Social programmes and people-oriented projects frequently fail due to mismanagement and poor targeting. This is often caused by the lack of adequate or properly used information.

As a rule, official and top-down data are used to identify the most vulnerable areas, and to allocate the available funds accordingly. Resources are allocated top-down from the central government to the states or regions, and from these to the municipalities. The municipalities (or the districts in large cities) are usually responsible for the actual transfer of these resources to the final beneficiaries. However, official and top-down data are not sufficient to detect the most vulnerable areas within municipalities or large districts. These are aggregated data, which tend to mask inequalities behind average values. When just these data are used, many poor areas are forgotten by decision-makers. The result is the unfair and inefficient allocation of the available resources.

We suggest that at the local level official information must be complemented with bottom-up data. A process approach can be very useful in this respect. However, elements from the blueprint approach must be adopted too, in order to make information generated at the community level supportive of decision-making.

The Case-Study

An innovative approach to information-handling was developed in Pau da Lima. For such an approach to work, an appropriate mix of elements respectively of the process and the blueprint type had to be adopted.

From our case-study we saw that a process, flexible approach was necessary to build up relevant knowledge about the local needs and characteristics of a poor urban and heterogeneous area such as Pau da Lima. Rapid appraisal methods proved to be particularly effective in this respect.

However, data so generated, in their raw form, could hardly support complex processes of decision-making at the managerial level. From that, the need arose to group the data into manageable categories, capable of expressing with precision relevant differences in local living conditions. Consequently, the available information was processed further, and the territory of the health district was subdivided into 'micro-areas' which represented relatively homogeneous geographic spaces in terms of living conditions. Moreover, a Geographic Information System was used to treat the information and analyse the spatial distribution of data. In order to facilitate the use of the system and to produce impact on decision-making, blueprint procedures were set for the analysis of data. In this way, the most vulnerable areas could be identified and prioritised with a high degree of precision, and tailor-made interventions could be designed to try to satisfy the needs of their residents.

Methodological Comments

This book is based on the analysis of a single case-study, which I analysed as a participant observer.

The choice of the case-study and the participant observation methodology were aimed at responding to a widely felt need – not so much that of broadening our knowledge of the processes of institutional development but, rather, of deepening it, in order to fill in the gap that still exists between theory and practice of management and implementation at the project level.[11] Qualitative research is usually indicated to analyse in-depth complex social organisations.[12] The participant observation allowed me to analyse 'from within' the implementation of the project of Pau da Lima.

In the case-study, however, analytical depth is usually gained at the expense of generalisation. This limitation was overcome to some extent, by analysing the context of the case-study, and making explicit the conditions under which the conclusions were valid. Moreover, comparisons were made over time, hence providing some evidence for testing hypotheses.

Structure of the Book

In Chapter 1 the terms are set for the theoretical question I am analysing. The main features are described of the process and the blueprint approach. Then, the necessity is discussed of integrating the main qualities of these two approaches – respectively, flexibility and specificity.

In Chapter 2 we discuss the relevance of these concepts for an operational problem that people-oriented projects have to face – the problem of creating a fit between knowledge-building about needs and decision-making about targets. We formulate the hypothesis that, for such a fit to be achieved, emphasis must be given respectively to flexibility in knowledge-building, and to specificity in decision-making. We formulate also a further hypothesis, that information-handling is a promising area for encouraging the achievement of this fit.

Chapter 3 describes the context of the project, from the macro level of policy-making and programmes, to the micro level of the project itself.

In Chapters 4 and 5 we analyse data collection and data processing for knowledge-building. We try to show that a process, flexible approach was necessary to collect relevant data about needs, but that elements from the blueprint approach had to be integrated with the latter to make the available information more precise and manageable.

In Chapter 6 the use of information for decision-making is analysed. We examine the impact of information on decision-making, and the quality of the decisions so produced. We argue that information was actually used, and the quality of decisions actually improved, due to the injection of blueprint rules in the decision-making process.

In the final chapter the conclusions of the case-study are drawn. The main findings of the analysis are compared with the initial assumptions and hypotheses, and the conditions are briefly discussed under which the conclusions seem to be valid.

NOTES

1. The project of Pau da Lima was a pilot project for the development of an innovative approach to information-handling for health district management. By the time this introduction has been written, about 60 municipalities in Brazil will be reproducing the methodologies initially developed in Pau da Lima, and similar projects will be under way in Peru, Colombia and Chile. These projects are sponsored by the Italian Cooperation and/or the Pan-American Health Organisation. In some of these projects these methodologies will be put into effect by social sectors other than health, in an intersectoral way. However, the data and the conclusions we report in this book refer to the case-study of Pau da Lima only.
2. F. Stewart, *Protecting the Poor during Adjustment in Latin America and the Caribbean in the 1980s. How Adequate was the World Bank Response*? (Turin/Oxford: Centro Studi Luca d'Agliano/Queen Elizabeth House Development Studies Working Papers 44, 1992), p. 14.
3. F. Stewart (1992), op. cit., p. 14a.
4. Examples in this respect are the Brazilian *Comunidade Solidária*, the Chilean *Fondo de Solidaridad y Inversión Social*, the Bolivian *Fondo de Emergencia Social*, the Colombian *Red de Solidaridad*, and the Mexican *Programa Solidaridad*.
5. M. Lipton and S. Maxwell, *The New Poverty Agenda: An Overview* (University of Sussex, Brighton: Institute of Development Studies Discussion Papers 306, 1992), p. 5.
6. World Bank, *World Development Report 1990* (Washington, DC: World Bank, 1990), and UNDP, *Human Development Report 1990* (Oxford: Oxford University Press, 1990).
7. World Bank, 1990, op.cit., p. 3.
8. C. Pinto, 'Injusto e Perverso', *Folha de São Paulo*, (3 March 1996), p. 19.
9. Ibid.
10. Ibid.
11. S. Paul, *Institutional Development in World Bank Projects: a Cross-Sectoral Review* (Washington, DC: World Bank, Policy, Research and External Affairs Working Papers, WP 392, 1990); J. Moris, *Managing Induced Rural Development* (Bloomington, IN: International Development Institute, 1981), p. 15; R. Heaver, *Bureaucratic Politics and Incentives in the Management of Rural Development* (Washington, DC: World Bank Staff Working Paper 537, 1982), p. 5.
12. G.J. McCall and J.L. Simmons (eds), *Issues in Participant Observation* (Reading MA: Addison-Wesley, 1969), p. 3; G. Rose, *Deciphering Sociological Research* (London: Macmillan, 1982), p. 108.

1

People-oriented Activities: From Blueprint and Process to Specificity and Flexibility

1.1 MANAGEMENT AND ADMINISTRATION IN LDCs

Both scholars and practitioners of development often encounter problems of organisation, management and administration, and we frequently read about the failure of mechanical transfers of western administrative theories and models to less developed countries (LDCs). This failure is often due to the fact that these models do not 'fit in' with different, complex, uncertain and variable local environments.

According to W.J. Siffin, it is very difficult to transfer administrative technologies successfully to LDCs – it works in exceptional circumstances, when such technologies can be buffered from their environment and replicated with little or no modifications:

> The long-established core technologies of public administration are palpable and specific in content and direct output. What to establish, how to establish it, with what probable outcomes, can be known in advance of action [...]. In technological activities, formalism and ambiguous bureaucratic behaviour frequently can be minimised, with gains in the effectiveness and predictability of particular bureaucratic domains.[1]

Similarly, Kiggundu *et al.* argue that conventional, Western-based models only work in LDCs when they focus on the 'technical core' of an organisation; they need profound modifications when they focus on the organisation's relationship with the environment. In the former case an organisation can function as a closed system, 'sealing its core technology from the intervention of "outside actors"'.[2]

In contrast, when an organisation cannot be sealed off from its environment – when it therefore cannot function according to standard technical procedures – the behaviour of individuals within it becomes less predictable. This may well affect the performance of the organisation as a whole.[3]

Patterns of individual behaviour seem to be strongly associated with the nature of the goods and services delivered. Different types of organisations require different kinds of institutional arrangements, as well as different incentives, to ensure the efficient production of goods and services.[4] The main distinction, here, is between more 'technical' organisations and those more concerned with 'people-oriented' activities.

When the goods/services delivered by a given organisation are of a technical nature – or when the focus is on the 'core technologies' of administration which are used to produce such goods or services – organisations in LDCs work in a way very similar to those in industrialised countries. As there is no need for interaction with the local environment, the individuals within such organisations can follow standard and almost universally valid procedures of organisational behaviour.

In contrast, when the dominant activities of organisations are people-oriented rather than technical, organisational behaviour differs between industrialised countries and LDCs. In this case interaction with the external environment (viz. its clients or beneficiaries) cannot be avoided, and the behaviour of individuals within organisations themselves is influenced by both the local value system and external interference. Only a degree of congruence between the organisational arrangements, the external environment, and the people within the organisation can then produce those incentives which would lead the people within the organisation to behave in the desired way.

1.2 BLUEPRINT AND PROCESS

This qualitative difference between 'technical' activities within organisations (those activities which deal with physical infrastructure construction, industrial plants, finance, etc.) and those which are 'people-oriented' (which deal with rural development, health, education, etc.) means that organisations require two distinct approaches to project management in these respective areas.[5] These approaches are usually referred to as the blueprint and the process approach. These should be understood as ideal types or as extremes of a continuum – although in reality field project management seldom fits in perfectly with the features of either of the approaches.

The blueprint approach to project management can be defined as follows:

- The project's goals are clearly stated at the outset. A complete preliminary analysis is carried out, in order to allocate resources and establish the functions, structures, tasks and norms which are required to attain the stated goals. Potential problems are also analysed in advance, and possible solutions are examined.[6]

- Projects are analysed and managed from a budgetary perspective, rather than from an organisational one.[7] Basically, only inputs and outputs are considered. Little attention is paid to those organisational elements which lie in between them.[8]

- Schedules for carrying out the planned activities are clearly defined, and implementation becomes just execution of these:[9] projects are merely conceived as vehicles for applying previously established plans.[10]

- The different phases of the project cycle – design, planning, implementation, monitoring and evaluation – are usually separated from each other, and the activities are broken down into component parts and executed separately according to already established procedures.[11]

- Monitoring and evaluation only aim at detecting if plans and schedules were followed – usually, there is little need for constant feedback to decision-makers, and for periodical adjustments of the course of the project.[12]

- Finally, executive and operational decision-making processes are characterised by a low degree of discretion, and the project's constituent units rarely need to enter into combined decision-making.[13]

In contrast, for those organisations which deal with people-oriented activities, and which deliver goods or services of a 'social' nature (health, education, rural development, institutional development etc.), a close interaction with the environment – especially with the prospective beneficiaries – is usually critical. For these organisations, then, the challenge is to find effective ways to deal with complexity, uncertainty and variability.

Projects for people-oriented organisational activities tend to emphasise the need for 'congruence' among different components of the organisation, and among these and the environment.[14] Attention must be paid to what happens beyond the formal boundaries of the organisation, and it may be necessary to negotiate and bargain with the relevant actors, such as clients, beneficiaries, politicians, and other organisations.[15] Most important of all, project managers should not try to get complete control of the environment – this would be an unattainable goal, due to the unpredictability of the latter.[16] Rather, they must try to regulate the interaction with it, by means of flexibility, experimentation, creativity, social learning, and decision-making by means of successive approximations.[17]

A process approach, then, tends to be recommended as the most appropriate to provide adequate institutional arrangements for people-oriented activities.[18] A blueprint approach is usually considered inappropriate for these activities, on the grounds that no plan can realistically define in advance duties and schedules, nor can it forecast the task performance and the way in which an organisation interacts with its environment in highly unpredictable and turbulent contexts.[19]

The main characteristics of the process approach to project management can be summarised as follows:

- Goals can be defined only in very general terms at the outset, as they must be adapted to emerging opportunities and obstacles; the organisational arrangements required for attaining them must also be defined gradually during project implementation and take account of the actual availability of resources and the reactions of the environment.[20]

- Planning and problem-solving are sequential and incremental[21] and based on social interaction, rather than on *a priori* analyses, because they take account of the purposive rather than mechanical nature of human behaviour; all the social actors (especially the beneficiaries) involved in a project must interact with each other, in order to share knowledge and resources.[22]

- A holistic view rather than analytic reductionism is required, as it is impossible to reduce complex problems into component parts for individual study.[23] Through social interaction it is possible to obtain a 'fit' between different project components, namely: beneficiary needs and programme output; programme task requirements and the distinctive competence of the organisation; the mechanisms for beneficiary demand expression and the decision processes of the organisation.[24] Moreover, knowledge-building, decision-making, and action-taking must be integrated rather than separated activities.[25]

- Monitoring is permanent, and feedback must be provided to decision-makers (social learning), in order to let them constantly readjust the course of the project. As the learning capacity of organisations is always limited, however, organisations are recommended to proceed sequentially, learning to be effective first, then efficient, and finally replicating their activities in wider contexts.[26]

Finally, if a blueprint approach were adopted in people-oriented activities, the likely result would be an anti-poor bias. The knowledge of the local reality available at the beginning of a project tends to be quite limited, as well as being influenced by those with special interests or local power. It is more difficult, then, for the poor and the excluded to make their needs and priorities visible at the beginning of a project.[27]

1.3 INTEGRATING BLUEPRINT AND PROCESS

The process theorists have the unequivocal merit to have shown that a pure rational and control-oriented approach to project management is based on a number of unrealistic and abstract assumptions. However, a 'pure' process approach is, in practice, hardly feasible: some elements from the blueprint approach are probably unavoidable, even in projects for people-oriented organisations. Ronald Dore argues that such projects have to reconcile two opposite needs, as

> [they] imply the need for spontaneity, flexibility, local initiative, decentralised decision-making. Yet the very idea of a community development *programme* involves deliberate planning, budgeting, rule-bound and even-handed decision-taking in the distribution of resources; in short, bureaucracy.[28]

Almost 30 years ago, Albert Hirschman concluded that most projects could be classified according to two major headings: the degree and types of uncertainties which characterise them, and the consequent degree of 'latitude' versus discipline to which project planners and operators are made subject.[29] Due to several uncertainties it is impossible to determine in advance all the future developments of a project. Unexpected threats to the success of a project appear, which are often offset, however, by equally unexpected solutions to them. Hirschman defines this as the principle of the 'hiding hand'. The 'hiding hand' is 'essentially a way of inducing action through error'.[30] Creativity, experimentation, and a sequential decision-making process are required in project management, to let this principle work. According to the degree of uncertainty, the participants in the project are allowed a variable degree of latitude in decision-making and individual behaviour. When latitude is absent or restricted, in turn, the participants' behaviour is made subject to discipline. A limited degree of latitude is not necessarily harmful to a project's success, as it allows, to some extent, the principle of the 'hiding hand' to work. An appropriate mix of latitude and discipline is to be recommended for most projects.

An explicit attempt to integrate blueprint and process is pursued by Brinkerhoff and Ingle. The authors suggest a 'structured flexibility approach', which 'integrates the blueprint model's planned structuring of action with the process model's flexibility and iterative learning orientation'.[31] This 'avoids the dysfunctional rigidities of blueprint management and systematises the fluidities of the process model's capacity-building aims'.[32] The proposed approach derives the orientation towards analysis, planning, and specificity from the blueprint model. However, it restricts the use of blueprint analytical tools, which are only utilised to clarify the degree of uncertainty of the context, and to develop initial actions, which are, subsequently, gradually modified. The participation of beneficiaries is identified as essential for the construction of the project's learning capacity. Moreover, the approach tries to integrate the long-term orientation towards capacity-building of the process model, with short-term service/product delivery targets.

We can conclude, then, that the adoption of a rationalistic, control-oriented, technology-driven approach (a blueprint approach), results in the excessive *rigidity* of a project, that is, in the inability to adapt flexibly the design of the institution which is being built, both to its external and internal environment. In contrast, those features which best identify the process approach – experimentation, bargaining, social interaction, incrementalism and so on – converge in stressing the need for *flexibility* and adaptation in a project for people-oriented organisations.

However, those authors who criticise a 'pure' process approach recognise the almost universal need for well-defined structures, tasks, and rules to guide the individual as well as the collective behaviour: they recognise the need to inject elements from the blueprint model in an overall process approach. The process theorists' almost exclusive emphasis on social interaction, community participation, and the 'soft' aspects of project management (that is, on the aspects of process proper), neglects certain 'hard', formal, or structural aspects of organisational behaviour, which are essential for action.[33]

The central problem thus is how to integrate these 'rigid' elements with the 'flexible' ones of the process approach. What essential qualities of the blueprint approach should be integrated with those of the process approach, and how can this integration be achieved without reducing the necessary, overall flexibility and capacity of adaptation of people-oriented activities within organisations? We shall try to answer this question, by considering, first, the role of individual incentives, and then, the role of technology in people-oriented activities.

Incentives in People-oriented Activities

The process theorists argue that a correct approach must be able to integrate 'learning' and 'action'; however, comparatively more attention has been paid to the 'learning' side of the process than to 'action'. We need to know how to transform the 'fluidities' of the learning process into institutionalised courses of action, so that individual tasks are performed with discipline and established institutional goals attained. Adequate organisational arrangements must be established; these, in turn, must be capable of orienting, by means of appropriate incentives, the behaviour of individuals within organisations.

It is precisely these aspects which the process approach tends to neglect. With its almost exclusive emphasis on flexibility and social interaction, it disregards the need for effective pressures to be put on individuals, in order to reduce the areas of vagueness and ambiguity within organisations.

These questions are approached from an illuminating perspective by Leibenstein. This author argues that the problem of the operational efficiency (X-efficiency) of organisations has mainly to do with the problem of individual motivation. To focus, as most economists do, on the relationship between input and output is not sufficient. The effective utilisation of an input depends on the adequate effort (Leibenstein defines it 'constraint concern') on the part of the individuals, that is, on the degree of motivational pressure which is put on the individuals themselves. Individuals respond rationally to the pressures – they calculate the disutility of an effort versus the utility of a good performance. Their performance depends on their job interpretation, which involves unavoidably some degree of 'latitude'. It is this job interpretation that managers must try to influence through appropriate incentives, so as to increase the effort of their subordinates.[34]

Appropriate incentives should originate *both* from social interaction and from adequate organisational arrangements. The former alone would produce signals too vague to put effective pressures on the participants; the latter are necessary to make these signals specific and precise enough to increase the effort or motivation of the participants. It is this second part aspect of incentive transmission which, in our opinion, is basically neglected in a pure process approach.

Technology and Discipline

Activities with a high technological content ('core technologies' of administration) seem to be capable of reducing the areas of vagueness in organisations. Not only their organisational design, but also the technology which lies at their core, imposes strict and standard rules of behaviour on the participants. That core technology operates according to a 'one-best-way', with little interaction with the external environment. In Leibenstein's terms, the technology puts effective motivational pressures on the individuals, thus increasing their 'constraint concern'.

Projects of this kind, with a high technological content, are the most suitable for the adoption of a blueprint approach. But this approach cannot be applied without substantial modifications to people-oriented activities. We must try, then, to isolate the basic qualities of such a technology-driven and control-oriented approach, and to assess, later on, if and to what extent they can be integrated with the basic hallmark of the process approach – flexibility.

The relationship between the nature of the technology which is employed by a project, and the incentives provided to the task performers (especially the managers), is analysed by Albert Hirschman[35] and Arturo Israel.[36] Both authors adopt a contingency model, focused on the nature of the technology utilised by different projects. These models are synthesised in Figure 1.1.

FIGURE 1.1
THE CONTINGENCY MODELS OF HIRSCHMAN AND ISRAEL[37]

Hirschman model:

Modern Technologies → Discipline → Modernising Behaviour → Success

Israel model:

Specificity of Technology (Goals + Methods + Control + Length of time) →
Specificity of Incentives (Intensity + Traceability + Spread + Immediacy of Effects) →
Success

In studies conducted 20 years apart, both authors recognise that the most successful projects are those which utilise modern technologies. These technologies, they argue, have a disciplinary effect on social behaviour.

According to Hirschman, modern technologies reduce the latitude in individual behaviour, and impose 'disciplines' which bring about modernising social behaviour. Israel develops this issue further: he identifies 'specificity' as the peculiar quality which gives the modern technology its disciplining power.[38] 'High-specificity' activities are those in which the goals, the methods to achieve them, and the procedures to control the achievements are clear and widely accepted. The outcomes of these activities are traceable, immediate, intense, and focused on a well-defined number of beneficiaries. Consequently, these outcomes can produce an effective feedback on those who manage them, allowing them to detect possible failures and their causes, and to correct the errors and improve performance – that is, they produce an incentive effect on decision-makers.

1.4 SPECIFICITY AND PEOPLE-ORIENTED ACTIVITIES

From the analysis of more than 200 World Bank institutional development projects in different sectors, Israel[39] concludes that the most successful are those in industry, telecommunications, some utilities, development finance companies or industrial development banks, and industrial types of agriculture such as plantations. Projects in other utilities, transport, and agricultural credit institutions record a middling performance. Finally, a low performance is registered in other types of agriculture, education, railways, integrated rural and urban development. Within institutions, those which deal with technical and financial issues score well; those which deal with planning, commercial activities, and extension perform no more than average; whereas projects which deal with training, maintenance, changes in organisational structures and processes, personnel management, interagency co-ordination, and sectorwide reform, tend to perform poorly. As far as project components are concerned, finally, the provision of equipment, or civil engineering works, perform well or fairly well, but service provision performs poorly. A good performance is recorded with regard to the provision of equipment; a medium one, with regard to civil engineering works; and a low one, with regard to service provision. Overall, people-oriented projects, those which are most directly related to the alleviation of poverty and which we previously assumed to be most suitable for the adoption of a process approach, tend to perform worst.

To explain these variations in project performance, Israel introduces the concepts of 'specificity' and 'competition'. It is the former which is quite relevant for the present discussion.

High specificity works as an incentive to the good performance of institutions and projects – it is defined as an ' "automatic" determinant of institutional performance'.[40] The degree of specificity is a characteristic inherent in the nature of the activities of projects and institutions, and the technology applicable to them. A high degree of specificity is found to be intrinsic to more technical activities, whereas a low degree of specificity is intrinsic to people-oriented activities.

Technical activities are highly specific, because they operate universally according to a one-best-way, and they leave little or no room for uncertainties, latitude, political interference, the emergence of informal goals or practices, and so on. All involved usually agree both on goals and on methods to achieve them. High-specificity, then, seems to be typical of those projects which (correctly) adopt a blueprint approach.[41]

People-oriented activities are low-specificity, and they tend to perform poorly. Improvement may be possible if stronger incentives are provided – yet, low-specificity activities are precisely those for which these incentives are more difficult to bring about. The spurious quantification of targets, the overspecification of tasks and rules of behaviour, and the application of strict control methods – that is, the adoption of a blueprint approach, typical of high-specificity activities – would be counterproductive, as it would merely increase the rigidity of people-oriented activities without improving their performance.

Israel suggests that this dilemma can be solved through appropriate managerial interventions. These can (artificially) reproduce specificity in people-oriented activities. Because they are non-mechanistic in nature, people-oriented activities tend to preserve much room for manoeuvre for managerial interventions. This room for manoeuvre should be used by managers to introduce some 'specificity surrogates' into the project – that is, to increase artificially the degree of specificity of the activities, without reducing their required flexibility. Israel makes various suggestions in this respect, such as:

- The simplification of the project goals, together with an optimal specification of the objectives of each function, without spurious quantification.
- Feedback from beneficiaries.
- The implementation of monitoring systems focused on key effects and capable of magnifying them.
- A few precise rules combined with a flexible management style.
- An organisational design through which higher-specificity activities exercise pressure on low-specificity ones.[42]

1.5 CONCLUSIONS: INTEGRATING SPECIFICITY AND FLEXIBILITY

In this chapter, we saw that the original trade-off between blueprint and process, from which our discussion originated, gradually evolved into a more definite problem – that of integrating flexibility and specificity in people-oriented activities. By isolating a single, synthetic, and crucial quality of the blueprint approach which is apparently missing in the process approach – specificity – we have tried to transform a set of logically contradictory prescriptions into a more manageable organisational problem. The operational question, now, becomes the following: in a project for people-oriented organisations, where should we try to increase, respectively, flexibility and specificity, and what tools from respectively the process and the blueprint approach could be used for this purpose?

In this book we shall try to answer these questions from the analysis of a case-study of an institutional development project in the health sector, in Salvador, Bahia, Brazil. We shall focus on the issues of information-handling and information systems. The main hypothesis which sustains the study is that these are promising areas for integrating specificity and flexibility through an appropriate mix of elements respectively of the blueprint and the process type.

The technological content of an activity determines, to some extent, its degree of specificity. Modern information technology, due to its broad applicability and tailor-made adaptation, expands the rank of potentially high-specificity activities – it represents an effective and widely usable specificity surrogate. More in general, technological change modifies the 'parameters' in this field. Such potentially positive developments, however, should not be taken for granted. One of the arguments we shall support in this study is that information systems cannot be treated as 'silver bullets'. Notwithstanding their potentially beneficial effects in terms of specificity, they cannot be adopted, implemented, and used irrespective of their contextual, institutional convenience. Above all, no information system can deliver its potentially rewarding outcomes, unless it is properly fed with relevant, good quality and manageable information.

NOTES

1. W.J. Siffin, 'Two Decades of Public Administration in Developing Countries', in L.D. Stifel, J.E. Black and J.S. Coleman (eds), *Education and Training for Public Sector Management in Developing Countries* (New York: The Rockefeller Foundation, Working Papers, 1977), pp. 56–7.
2. M.N. Kiggundu, J.J. Jorgensen and T. Hafsi, 'Administrative Theory and Practice in Developing Countries: A Synthesis', *Administrative Science Quarterly*, 28 (1983), p. 79.
3. P. Blunt, 'Strategies for Enhancing Organisational Effectiveness in the Third World', *Public Administration and Development*, 10 (1990), pp. 299–313.

4. J.S. Wunsch, 'Sustaining Third World Infrastructure Investments: Decentralization and Alternative Strategies', *Public Administration and Development*, 11 (1991), pp. 5–23.
5. C.F. Sweet and P. Wiesel, 'Process vs. Blueprint Models for Designing Rural Development Projects', in G. Honadle and R. Klauss (eds), *International Development Administration. Implementation Analysis for Development Projects* (New York: Praeger Special Studies, 1979), pp. 127–45.
6. C.F. Sweet and P. Wiesel (1979), op.cit., pp. 129–30; J. Moris, *Managing Induced Rural Development* (Bloomington IN: International Development Institute, 1981), pp. 19–20.
7. J. Moris (1981), op. cit., p. 20.
8. J. Moris, *What Organisation Theory Has to Offer Third World Agricultural Managers* (London: ODI, undated), p. 21.
9. J. Moris (undated), op. cit., p. 25.
10. C.F. Sweet and P. Wiesel (1979), op.cit., p. 130.
11. J. Moris (1981), op. cit., p. 20.
12. J. Moris (undated), op. cit., p. 21.
13. J. Moris (undated), op. cit., p. 27.
14. S. Paul, 'The Strategic Management of Development Programmes: Evidence from an International Study', *International Review of Administrative Sciences*, 49, 1 (1983a), p. 76; S. Paul, *Strategic Management of Development Programmes: Guidelines for Action*, (Geneva: ILO, Management Development Series N° 19, 1983b), p. 2.
15. D.W. Brinkerhoff and R. Klauss, 'Managerial roles for social development management', *Public Administration and Development*, 5, 2 (1985), pp. 149–52.
16. See M. Landau and R. Stout, Jr, 'To Manage Is Not To Control: Or the Folly of Type II Errors', *Public Administration Review*, 39, 2 (March/April 1979) pp. 148–56. If the central role of managers is conceived as dealing with uncertainty, then managers should not be primarily concerned with control. A control-oriented process of rational calculation is effective only where both goals and the instruments to achieve them are relatively certain. Under other contingencies, Moris suggests managers should rely upon negotiation, judgement, or even inspiration. See J. Moris (undated), op. cit., p.10, quoting J.D. Thompson, *Organisations in Action* (New York: Mc Graw-Hill, 1967).
17. D.A. Rondinelli, 'The Dilemma of Development Administration: Complexity and Uncertainty in Control-Oriented Bureaucracies', *World Politics*, 35, 1 (1982), pp. 43–72; D.A. Rondinelli, *Development Projects as Policy Experiments* (London: Methuen, 1983).
18. D.C. Korten, 'Community Organisation and Rural Development, a Learning Process Approach', *Public Administration Review*, 40, 5, (1980), pp. 481–511; D.C. Korten, 'The Management of Social Transformation', *Public Administration Review*, 41 (Nov.–Dec. 1981), pp. 609–18; R. Chambers, *Rural Development: Putting the Last First* (London: Longman, 1983); N. Uphoff, 'Participatory Evaluation of Farmer Organizations' Capacity for Development Tasks', *Agricultural Administration and Extension*, 30, (1988), pp. 43–64; D.W. Brinkerhoff and R. Klauss (1985), op. cit.; G. Gran, *Development by People* (New York: Praeger, 1983).

19. J. Moris (undated), op. cit., p. 27.
20. C.F. Sweet and P. Wiesel (1979), op.cit., pp. 130 and 144.
21. See C.E. Lindblom, 'The Science of Muddling Through', *Public Administration Review*, 29, (1959), pp. 79–99, and C.E. Lindblom, 'The Sociology of Planning: Thought and Social Interaction', in M. Bornstein (ed.), *Economic Planning East and West* (Cambridge MA: Ballinger Publishing Company, 1975), pp. 23–60. The studies of Lindblom on the decision-making process, and his suggestions in favour of an incrementalist perspective, have exercised a strong influence on the process approach as a whole. According to Lindblom, complex social problems have to be approached from a social-interactive rather than a purely rational perspective. In his view, the role of social interaction is the opposite of that conceived by the blueprint approach – it can provide solutions to problems, rather than being a disturbance of purely 'rational' planning processes. Rational analysis must be directed at understanding the others, influencing them, and designing the procedures which regulate the interaction processes. The competence to plan is a scarce resource, which has to be carefully allocated and not overcommitted. He prescribes a method of planning called 'disjointed incrementalism', characterised by: (a) the limitation of analysis to alternative policies only incrementally different from prevailing policies; (b) the conversion of 'the problem' into a sequence of problems; and (c) the examination of goals or values in close connection with, rather than prior to, the empirical investigation of policy alternatives and their possible consequences (Lindblom, 1975, op. cit., pp. 46–7).
22. D.C. Korten (1981), op. cit., pp. 612–13; D.C. Korten, 'Rural Development Programming: The Learning Process Approach', in D.C. Korten and R. Klauss (eds), *People-centred development: contributions towards theory and planning frameworks* (West Hartford CT: Kumarian Press, 1984), p. 182.
23. D.C. Korten (1981), op. cit., p. 612.
24. D.C. Korten (1980), op. cit., p. 495; D.C. Korten (1984), op. cit., p. 181.
25. D.C. Korten (1984), op. cit., p. 182.
26. D.C. Korten (1980), op. cit, p. 500; D.C. Korten (1984), op. cit., p. 183.
27. R. Chambers, *Normal Professionalism and the Early Project Process: Problems and Solutions* (University of Sussex, Brighton: IDS Discussion Paper 247, 1988b), p. 5.
28. R. Dore, 'Community Development in the 1970s', in R. Dore and Z. Mars (eds), *Community Development* (London/Paris: Croon Helm/UNESCO, 1981), p. 39.
29. A.O. Hirschman, *Development Projects Observed* (Washington, DC: Brookings Institutions, 1967). Hirschman defines 'latitude' as 'the characteristic of a project (or task) that permits the project planners and operators to mold it, or let it slip, in one direction or another, regardless of outside occurrences' (Hirschman, 1967, op. cit., p. 86).
30. A.O. Hirschman (1967), op. cit., p. 29.
31. D.W. Brinkerhoff and M.D. Ingle, 'Integrating Blueprint and Process: a Structured Flexibility Approach to Development Management', *Public Administration and Development*, 9 (1989), p. 487.
32. D.W. Brinkerhoff and M.D. Ingle (1989), op.cit., p. 491.

33. In general, the process approach has been influenced by the revolt against positivistic epistemology, led by the phenomenologists and the ethnomethodologists against the structural-functionalists in the late 1960s and early 1970s. A detailed analysis of this paradigm change, specifically in relation to organisational theory, can be found in M. Reed, *Redirections in Organizational Analysis* (London: Tavistock, 1985). According to this author, the structural-functionalist theory of organisations was initially criticised on the grounds that social interaction within organisations was seen from an exclusively behaviourist point of view; instead, a hermeneutic perspective was proposed, focused on the actors' subjectively meaningful interpretation of social reality – organisations should be analysed as 'negotiated social orders'. Eventually, however, this fruitful action perspective evolved into that of the ethnomethodologists, with its exclusive emphasis on social interaction and negotiation, the refusal of scientific knowledge in favour of commonsense, and the dissolution of the concept of formal, structural organisation.
34. H. Leibenstein, *Beyond Economic Man: a New Foundation for Micro-economics* (Cambridge, MA: Harvard University Press, 1976), p. 123.
35. A. O. Hirschman (1967), op. cit.
36. A. Israel, *Institutional Development. Incentives to Performance* (Baltimore: Johns Hopkins University Press, 1987).
37. D.K. Leonard, *Workshops on Organisational Analysis* (University of Sussex, Brighton: notes for the IDS Seminars, June 1991).
38. Ibid.
39. A. Israel (1987), op. cit., pp. 19–26.
40. A. Israel (1987), op. cit., p.49.
41. Israel gives the following example of activities with a different degree of specificity. The maintenance of a jet engine is a typical high-specificity activity. There is universal agreement about the way in which jet engine maintenance has to be done. Precise functions are specified, operationalised into well-defined procedures, and assigned to specific tasks. When these tasks are performed badly, the effects are immediate (for instance the plane crashes), well-focused and intense (a given number of people die), and traceable (bad maintenance can be pinpointed as the cause of failure). In contrast, educational counselling is a typical low-specificity activity. In educational counselling targets cannot be defined with precision; the way in which the counsellor should act with each student is highly variable; the effects of either good or bad counselling can hardly be isolated from the effects of other contextual factors, and can take a long time to become manifest. See A. Israel (1987), op. cit., pp. 49–50.
42. A. Israel, op. cit., pp.152–3.

2

Knowledge-Building, Decision-Making and Information-Handling: An Introduction to the Case-study of Pau da Lima

2.1 INTRODUCTION

The object of analysis of our study is an innovative approach to information-handling which has been developed in a pilot health district project in Salvador, Bahia, Brazil. In this chapter we introduce the case-study, approaching the question of the 'fit' between knowledge-building and decision-making in complex organisations dealing with people-oriented activities. Knowledge-building and decision-making seem to induce contradictory needs in these organisations. The former often implies the establishment of adequate channels for needs expression. Usually the beneficiaries' needs are not known in advance, and can be best detected by means of flexible and participatory methods of data collection – that is, by adopting an overall process approach. However, this approach seems to be less appropriate when information generated at the community level has to be used to effectively support complex processes of decision-making at the managerial level. For that, analytical methods are usually required, often supported by sophisticated technologies and filled in with some specialised, technical knowledge. These methods are quite typical of a blueprint approach, and their adoption aims at increasing the degree of specificity of the decision-making processes.

Information-handling for knowledge-building and decision-making is a relevant object of analysis, as elements from respectively the process and the blueprint approach have to be mixed in it. In our study, we shall try to show to what extent and how these elements were successfully integrated in the project of Pau da Lima. In other words, we shall discuss how information generated at the community level through flexible and participatory methods was gradually transformed, and then used at the managerial level, in order to support decision-making, becoming an effective specificity surrogate.

2.2 KNOWLEDGE-BUILDING AND DECISION-MAKING IN COMPLEX ORGANISATIONS

A health district (or local health system) is a complex organisational entity. In a health district both knowledge-building and decision-making are critical issues.

The concept of local health system has been widely used by the Pan American Health Organisation (PAHO). A local health system is a decentralised entity, fully integrated with the rest of the health sector, capable of detecting the health needs of its constituency, fairly democratic and open to the participation of the community, as well as apt to co-ordinate different local resources (from both within and outside the health sector) in an inter-sectoral way.[1]

A health district is supposed to be a demand-driven institution. Moreover, it is a complex organisation, as it must (a) detect the health needs coming bottom-up from its constituency, (b) translate top-down health policies into a form which is appropriate to the specific conditions of its constituency, and (c) integrate the different, local health resources, so as to respond efficiently and effectively to such needs.[2]

In all people-oriented (or demand-driven) organisations, a 'fit' has to be achieved between the way in which the clientele demands are expressed and the way in which the institution's decision-making process is organised.[3] For the institutional development of a health district the search of this fit is a crucial goal.

However, achieving this fit is not an easy task. Specific and differentiated needs, respectively for knowledge-building and decision-making, have to be met.

In Chapter 1 we saw that in situations of complexity and uncertainty, typical of people-oriented activities, a process approach is recommended. According to this approach, social interaction should be the means through which knowledge-building and decision-making are linked in a successive approximation process.

With specific reference to knowledge-building, the presence of effective channels through which clients can express their needs is crucial. However, these channels are not always available. Data on clients' needs and characteristics are often scarce, unreliable, or biased. For instance, information on health needs based only on those data available to the health centres could be quite biased, as this expresses the epidemiological profile merely of those people who actually have access to health-care services, rather than of the population as a whole. Socio-economic and environmental data are often unreliable and out of date, for areas which experience a rapid urbanisation through successive waves of immigration – as is the case for urban, peripheral health districts. These data have to be considered, if a concept of 'health need' wider than the purely clinical one has to be adopted.[4] Moreover, the bias which derives from the lack of complete data implies that it is often the needs of the most disadvantaged and marginalised groups that are denied any possibility of expression.[5] This is a particularly serious problem if we assume – as the local health system proposal does – a commitment to equity.[6]

For all these reasons, it is often necessary for the health district to collect fresh information from the field, if clientele needs are to find expression. However, a systematic analysis of these needs conducted through orthodox methods – such as well-structured surveys on representative samples of the population – are long and expensive. Hence, the use of 'quick and reasonably clean' methods of data collection is often required for overcoming these difficulties.[7]

More specifically, the use of participatory methods of data collection has been suggested by several supporters of the process approach.[8] These methods, in fact, can provide reasonable information in a short time and at low costs. They tend also to stimulate the participation of the local population in the definition of its own needs, hence fostering a process of social interaction between institutions and beneficiaries. In this respect, Korten argues that local officers and the community must share knowledge and continuously get engaged in experimenting with new and simple methods of data collection.[9] According to Chambers, the project identification cannot be 'a one-shot event, but an adaptive sequence of finding out what best to do'.[10] Moreover, through a holistic approach these methods can embrace the different points of view which are expressed by a heterogeneous community – they can perceive 'local diversity';[11] most important of all, they can embrace also the point of view of the 'unseen and the unknown'.[12]

One can hardly deny the potential of flexible, participatory methods of data collection and social interaction for knowledge-building in people-oriented activities. However, we believe that opposing these methods to an analytic or scientific approach is incorrect.[13] Such an opposition is expressed clearly by some process theorists. For instance, Korten argues that the use of these methods involves 'informed interpretation of the reality rather than extensive statistical analysis [...] narrative rather than numerical presentations';[14] consequently, he rejects scientific knowledge, because of its logic based on 'analytic reductionism which proceeds by reducing complex problems into component parts for individual study'.[15] Lindblom, in turn, defines 'social interaction as an alternative to thought'.[16]

All these arguments seem to converge in emphasising the local, natural knowledge of the community and, consequently, in proposing to build up knowledge for decision-making which stresses synthesis instead of analysis, oral rather than written communication, argumentation rather than explanation, analogic or heuristic methods rather than more rigorous or scientific ones, and iterative processes rather than discrete activities.

One can question, however, to what extent these participatory and process methods of data collection alone, based on social interaction, can support the elaborate procedures of decision-making that are necessary for managing complex organisations: hence, if they can actually support the gradual establishment of an appropriate fit between knowledge-building and decision-making.

It is likely that, for 'needs expression' to become 'knowledge', data generated from the field have to pass through some analytical procedure. The point, then, is to simplify these procedures so as to make them manageable – analytical and statistical methods tend to be sophisticated and management-intensive, and therefore not appropriate for those institutions which are provided with a weak administrative capacity.

In order to deal with this point, we have to consider more in depth the second issue of Korten's model, the other side of his fit, namely how a complex, people-oriented organisation should organise its process of decision-making.

With specific reference to health districts, planning and programming are complex as well as technical activities; these demand the complementary adoption of an analytic approach.

According to Veronesi, health district management implies both a strategic function (determination of the goals of the health district) and an administrative one (organisation and execution of the technical activities necessary for achieving such goals).[17] Both functions are complex ones. The former function requires the concentration of intelligence and a strategic vision at the top of the system; the latter, the use of specialised, professional knowledge. On the one hand, planning implies prioritising precise targets, both in terms of the health problems to attack, and in terms of the social groups on which to concentrate the activities. On the other hand, programming implies several choices about the resources to mobilise, the way in which to achieve co-ordination and synergy between different types of resource-providers, and the technologies to use, together with an appraisal in terms of political, economic and technical feasibility of the proposed interventions.

Decisions on these issues have to be taken as health care supply is always a scarce commodity in relation to demand.[18] Hence, decisions must be taken about what aspects of such demand should be given priority, and how they should be satisfied.

Therefore, we can agree with Korten when he suggests identifying 'target group members and behaviours in terms relevant to program action rather than simply producing aggregated statistics',[19] as statistical data per se may not be relevant. Nevertheless, we cannot assume that the 'informed interpretations of the reality' that he recommends automatically lead to such a target identification: some more steps, often of an analytical or technical nature, are necessary to get to this. Similarly, we do agree on the need to 'facilitate local level decision-making through exchange and bargaining processes'.[20] But we must also be aware that there is a risk of getting engaged in a never ending, circular process of bargaining, unless such a process is framed by and structured around precise alternatives of action. This, in turn, implies that the available information must provide the participants with precise indications about the possible courses of action.

For planning and management, then, it is not sufficient to detect needs and demands: these have to be transformed into goals and plans for action – and such a transformation is likely to require some sort of analysis and the application of specialised techniques.

A holistic and participatory approach can be necessary, then, to deal with complex situations. But the purpose of knowledge-building for decision-making is the reduction of this complexity, to some extent through standardisation and simplification. Chambers indicates centralisation, standardisation and simplification as normal tendencies of field bureaucracies, responsible for its difficulty to deal with local diversity.[21] We tend to argue, nonetheless, that without at least some degree of simplification and standardisation, these bureaucracies could not work at all. What is crucial, however, is *how* standardisation and simplification are obtained – whether by reducing artificially the local complexity, or by taking account properly of it.

In conclusion, the problem we are facing is if it is possible (and how) to integrate participatory, bottom-up, interpretative methods of knowledge-building (typical of a process approach) with analytic, top-down methods and the application of specialised, technical and professional knowledge (typical features of the blueprint approach), in order to support decision-making effectively, and to increase the degree of specificity of people-oriented activities. In practical terms, this is a problem of building up knowledge which is, at the same time, relevant, manageable, and capable of providing decision-makers with precise indications or 'signals' about goals, targets and possible alternatives of action. Information – as a potential specificity surrogate – is an important part of such 'signals'.

2.3 INFORMATION-HANDLING FOR KNOWLEDGE-BUILDING AND DECISION-MAKING

Information is a crucial issue for both knowledge-building and decision-making.

With reference to the problem of the fit between clients' demands and organisation's decisions, information systems seem to represent a promising area for innovations. This point is expressed clearly by Chambers:

> The more general question for normal bureaucracy is whether it can incorporate and service local needs and demands through search. Often senior staff will not welcome or support demands from below, but incentive and reward systems might be reoriented to recognise and reward such upward requests. One difficulty would be the extra work involved. The prestige and effectiveness of new information systems could help here.[22]

However, what emerges from a brief review of the literature on information systems in LDCs is a generalised incapacity to use effectively the information which is being produced, especially at the local level.

Several inadequacies of current health information systems are reported by de Kadt; among them, the extreme burden represented by over-sophisticated information, the over-centralisation and excessive aggregation of data, and – most serious of all – the 'failure to analyse the available information adequately or to use it for planning or feedback'.[23] Therefore, it is stated, health information systems need simplification, and, in particular, a plea is made so that 'much more serious attention is paid to the processes and procedures through which information can become an effective ingredient in planning and implementation – to health information management'.[24]

Similar arguments are advanced by Chanawongse and Singhadej, who complain about the fact that 'information systems, their organisation and their maintenance are oriented towards information generation rather than information usage'.[25]

Marcus Ingle, in turn, concludes a review of the management application of computerised information systems in LDCs by stating that the lack of timely and quality information, which managers would be able to use in decision-making, tends to separate the managers themselves from the work context and to create distrust towards information itself. This produces a vicious circle responsible for an even lesser use of information in the adaptation of the operations.[26]

In a study on the use of different computerised information systems in Kenya, Peterson distinguishes between 'analysing applications' and 'processing applications' of these systems. In this study it is stated that processing applications are relatively simple, as they involve a mere throughput of data. In contrast, analysing applications are more complex and include data assembly, sensitivity analysis, and modelling.[27]

Information needs for managing the activities of a health district are of the 'analysing application' rather than the 'processing application' type. Managing such a complex organisation, as we mentioned previously, implies the capacity to identify needs and resources and to match one with another. This implies, in turn, an analytical exercise – assembling and recombining data, crossing them, using them for predicting scenarios, and so on – rather than a mere, automatic processing of data themselves.

The conclusions of Peterson's study point out that the use of information systems for the purpose of analysis rather than for the mere automation of data processing is difficult in development bureaucracies because of the lack of training and motivation; other constraints are represented by the limited supply of relevant information and the lack of demand for analysis by decision-makers.

The way in which information is usually collected and presented seems particularly unsuited to its analytical use. Often a profusion of data, with little or no analytical relevance, is produced, and then not used to support decision-making. This means that information is not used, because it does not perform either of the functions whose importance we have previously stressed: it neither expresses local needs, nor does it support – in a simplified way – decision-making. Then, if information is not used, this is because it is either useless, or too complex, or both. In other words, all too often information is neither *relevant* nor *manageable*. Data, in this sense, are not turned into information: as Conyers and Hills put it, in fact, 'the nature and form of data determine their value as information for a particular decision-making purpose'.[28] It is to this 'form and nature', then, that we now turn.

In a health district, the problem of the *relevance* of information for planning and management is at least partially related to the lack of disaggregated, first-hand data concerning clientele needs. Data about the availability of resources, the production and productivity of services (unfortunately not about costs) are generally produced – even in excess. In contrast, data about health needs – which assume the notion of need or risk in a wider sense than the strictly clinical one – disaggregated below the district level, are seldom available. As we previously discussed, participatory methods of research can contribute to build up relevant knowledge on local needs. However, they do not necessarily foster the manageability of information.

The problem of the *manageability* of information, in fact, seems to refer mainly to the excessive burden that a huge amount of data to be analysed represents especially for the local level. Quite often these data are not standardised, so that crossing or making comparisons among them becomes virtually impossible. Therefore it becomes crucial to increase the institution's capacity to analyse the available information: this can be achieved by limiting the amount of data to be analysed, and making information more comprehensible. In turn, this requires making data more immediately comparable, allowing data crossing in a quick, simple and visible form, and letting problems and resources be associated in such a way that one can easily see if and how they can be matched with each other.

Information, then, must be manageable enough to provide planners with precise, visual and intuitive indications about priorities and alternatives of actions. It must put some sort of 'pressure' to reduce the inherent degree of 'latitude' of decision-making in people-oriented activities – only in this sense, can information be effectively supportive of the latter, and so become a specificity surrogate. Even so, 'raw' data produced by participatory methods – which are extremely helpful in building up relevant knowledge on local needs – cannot provide formal, immediate inputs to decision-making: in order to provide this kind of pressure, information has to be appropriately treated and transformed.

2.4 INFORMATION-HANDLING IN PAU DA LIMA

The main products of the project of Pau da Lima are an innovative approach to information-handling and an information system which supports it. These products are the consequence of the search, by the project management, for a fit between knowledge-building and decision-making.

The information system is a GIS (Geographic Information System), fed with data generated at the community level through rapid, participatory methods.[29] The system aims to turn information into a specificity surrogate, improving the decisions taken at the health district managerial level. This is meant to be achieved by increasing the *disaggregation of data* and improving the capacity of *analysis of the spatial distribution* of different information.

Field research conducted at the beginning of the project through rapid appraisal procedures showed very clearly that dramatic inequalities in living and health conditions were masked by the aggregated data which had been used so far. Data disaggregation, then, became a prerequisite for allowing decision-makers to detect the most disadvantaged groups and plan well-targeted interventions towards them. Data disaggregation was conducted in order to make more comprehensible the heterogeneous and complex reality of the district.

The health district, then, was divided into smaller areas, called health centre's responsibility areas (HCRAs). This division was obtained by considering the population's patterns of access to, and use of, the health centres. HCRAs are the operative units of the district's health system. So data were disaggregated in order to facilitate their management. The aim was to allow managers to compare the health conditions of different HCRAs and thus improve the allocative capacity of the health district.

Moreover, every HCRA was in due course further divided into smaller areas, called micro-areas, as it became clear that even HCRAs could be highly heterogeneous areas, because their urbanisation had often taken place through successive waves of immigration, thus creating areas of relative welfare next to slums and squatters. The division into micro-areas respects the 'social' limits of settlements; in other words, the inhabitants of a given micro-area share broadly similar living conditions – they have similar levels of household income, housing conditions, sanitation, and so on – and are therefore in most cases exposed to reasonably homogeneous health hazards. The division into micro-areas was obtained by analysing the data collected through the rapid appraisal methods. As the micro-areas were defined by considering the living conditions of the resident population, they represent a manageable proxy for identifying and locating different social groups or strata in the territory. The aim of this further disaggregation of data was to provide precise indications to decision-makers, and to allow them to detect in a simplified way physically reachable target groups within each HCRA. This, in turn, was meant to make the health district management capable of acting with positive discrimination – to concentrate resources where the need is greatest – and consequently to increase the impact of its interventions.

Moreover, the information system was designed so as to allow managers to adapt such interventions to their specific contexts; the GIS, in fact, permits to 'zoom in' to the selected micro-areas or enlarge them, and consider in detail their characteristics (local risks and resources). In this respect, the capacity to analyse the spatial distribution of different information was seen as crucial. By overlaying different data bases to the same geographic space (single micro-areas), it became possible to observe in a visual and intuitive way the spatial distribution of ill-health events, and to relate them to social determinants located in the territory, such as environmental hazards, lack of piped water, precarious housing,

TABLE 2.1
INFORMATION-HANDLING IN KNOWLEDGE-BUILDING AND DECISION-MAKING IN PAU DA LIMA

FEATURES OF INFORMATION HANDLING	KNOWLEDGE-BUILDING (community level)	DECISION-MAKING (managerial level)
Information system	community networks	GIS
Methods of data handling	Qualitative	Quantitative
Cognitive approach	Synthetic, descriptive, holistic	Analytical, explanatory, simplified
Equipment used	Maps, questionnaires	Computers
Communication flows	Bottom-up	Top-down
Production of information-handling	Expression of needs	Prioritisation of targets and definition of actions
Main actors	Key informants from	Managers and

etc. The aim, then, was to support intersectoral action and to direct priority to preventive (that is, people-oriented) measures rather than medical procedures.

In Pau da Lima, information generated for knowledge-building has been gradually transformed, in order to make it more supportive of decision-making. Different tools, methods, and approaches have been used for treating information, respectively for knowledge-building and decision-making. This means that different and even opposed features characterise respectively knowledge-building and decision-making in the Pau da Lima project, as Table 2.1 indicates.

As we can see from Table 2.1, information-handling in Pau da Lima shows, at the stage of knowledge-building, some typical features of the process approach – it is generated at the community level and from community networks, is mainly qualitative, adopts a holistic approach, and emphasises bottom-up communication and needs expression.

At the stage of decision-making, instead, information presents different features, quite characteristic of the blueprint approach – it incorporates a high technological content, is mainly quantitative, is oriented towards analysis, and emphasises top-down communication flows and the prioritisation of targets.

The 'blueprint vs. process' dilemma emerged quite clearly, in the project of Pau da Lima, with regard to information-handling. Bottom-up methods of data collection were used to bolster the flexibility and capacity of adaptation of the health district to the variable and heterogeneous needs of its beneficiaries; analytical tools, in contrast, were used to support decision-making for defining clear goals and clear means for attaining them. Bottom-up information was treated, then, so as to represent a specificity surrogate for decision-making.

NOTES

1. See PAHO, *Documento CD 33/14, Resolución XV–XXXIII del Comité Directivo* (Washington: PAHO 1988).
2. E. Veronesi, *Relazione sulla missione presso la Segreteria della Sanità dello Stato di Bahia* (Rome: mimeo, 1989).
3. D.C. Korten, 'Rural Development Programming: The Learning Process Approach', in D.C. Korten and R. Klauss (eds), *People-centred development: contributions towards theory and planning frameworks* (West Hartford, CT: Kumarian Press, 1984), p. 181.
4. E. de Kadt and R. Tasca, *Promovendo a Equidade: Um Novo Enfoque com Base no Setor Saúde* (São Paulo: Hucitec/Cooperação Italiana em Saúde, 1993), pp. 22–5. The English version is also available: *Promoting Equity: A New Approach from the Health Sector* (Washington, DC: PAHO, 1993).
5. D.A. Rondinelli, 'The Dilemma of Development Administration: Complexity and Uncertainty in Control-Oriented Bureaucracies', *World Politics*, 35, 1 (1982), p. 56.
6. E.V. Mendes, 'Importancia de los Sistemas Locales de Salud en la Transformación de los Sistemas Nacionales de Salud', in J.M. Paganini and R. Capote Mir (eds), *Los Sistemas Locales de Salud: Conceptos, Métodos, Experiencias* (Washington DC: PAHO, Scientific Publication 519, 1990), pp. 24–5.
7. D. Conyers and P. Hills, *An Introduction to Development Planning in the Third World* (Chichester, New York, Brisbane, Toronto, Singapore: John Wiley and Sons, 1984), p. 103.
8. D.C. Korten (1984), op. cit., p. 186; R. Chambers, 'Rapid Rural Appraisal: Rationale and Repertoire', *Public Administration and Development*, 1 (1981), pp.95–106; R. Chambers, 'Bureaucratic Reversals and Local Diversity', *IDS Bulletin*, 19, 4 (1988a), p. 55; R. Chambers, *Normal Professionalism and the Early Project Process: Problems and Solutions* (University of Sussex, Brighton: IDS Discussion Paper 247, 1988b), p. 13; R. Chambers, *Rural*

Development: Putting the Last First (London: Longman, 1983), p. 200; R. Longhurst (ed.), 'Rapid Rural Appraisal', *Bulletin of the Institute of Development Studies*, 12, 4 (1981).

9. D.C. Korten (1984), op. cit., p. 186.
10. R. Chambers (1988b), op. cit., p. 12.
11. R. Chambers (1988a), op. cit., p. 55.
12. R. Chambers (1983), op. cit., p. 23.
13. One must not confuse the legitimate refusal of certain extreme, positivist positions, with a more general (and not legitimate) anti-scientism. The adoption of a scientific (that is, rigorous) approach does not necessarily imply the submission to a rigid, hypothetico-deductive method of investigation. For a plea in favour of more epistemological 'eclecticism' in medical geography – a subject which is relevant to the approach developed in Pau da Lima – see J.D. Mayer, 'Challenges to Understanding Spatial Patterns of Disease: Philosophical Alternatives to Logical Positivism', *Social Science and Medicine*, 35, 4 (1992), pp. 579–87, and D. Bennett, 'Explanation in Medical Geography: Evidence and Epistemology', *Social Science and Medicine*, 33, 4 (1991), pp. 339–46.
14. D.C. Korten (1984), op. cit., p. 186.
15. D.C. Korten, 'The Management of Social Transformation', *Public Administration Review*, 41, (Nov.–Dec. 1981), p. 612.
16. C.E. Lindblom, 'The Sociology of Planning: Thought and Social Interaction', in M. Bornstein (ed.), *Economic Planning East and West* (Cambridge, MA: Ballinger Publishing Company, 1975), p. 30.
17. E. Veronesi, op. cit., 1989.
18. Ibid.
19. D.C. Korten (1984), op. cit., p. 186.
20. D.C. Korten (1981), p. 613.
21. R. Chambers (1988a), op. cit., p. 51.
22. R. Chambers (1988a), op. cit., pp. 55–6.
23. E. de Kadt, 'Making Health Policy Management Intersectoral: Issues of Information Analysis and Use in Less Developed Countries', *Social Science and Medicine*, 29, 4 (1989), p. 506.
24. Ibid.
25. Aga Khan Foundation, *Management Information Systems and Microcomputers in Primary Health Care* (Lisbon: report of an international workshop, Nov. 1987), p. 34.
26. M.D. Ingle, *Evaluating the Appropriateness of Microcomputers for Management Applications in Developing Countries* (New York: Development Project Management Centre, 1983), p. 40.
27. S.B. Peterson, *From Processing to Analyzing: Intensifying the Use of Microcomputers in Development Bureaucracies* (Cambridge, MA: Harvard Institute for International Development, Development Discussion Paper, 1990a), p. i.
28. D. Conyers and P. Hills (1984), op. cit., p. 88.

29. GIS are information systems in which data bases (attributes) are related to geographic entities in digital maps. A GIS can be defined as a 'system of hardware, software and procedures designed to support the capture, management, manipulation, analysis, modelling and display of spatially referenced data for solving complex planning and management problems.' Automated Methods, *ReGIS/ReGEO User's Guide (*Republic of South Africa: Automated Methods Pty. Ltd., 1995), p. 1.1.

3

The Pilot Project of Pau da Lima: Its Context and Characteristics

3.1 INTRODUCTION: THE REFORM OF THE NATIONAL HEALTH SYSTEM IN BRAZIL

The implementation of health districts in Brazil was part of the wider process of reform of the national health system (NHS).

The reform was meant to put into practice the principles of universality and equity in health care which had been established by the Constitution of 1988. However, the reform process was implemented at different rates of speed in different states of Brazil, according to the local political situation and administrative capacity.

At the end of 1990 the law 8080/1990 was approved which was intended to regulate and foster the reform process. This law actually helped to stimulate the unification and decentralisation of the health care system, which had been made up, so far, of different health care providers, respectively from the federal, state, and municipal level. The unification and decentralisation of the NHS were meant to improve the efficiency of health care services, and to make them closer to the people. However, even this law did not define clearly to what extent and how the system should be reoriented to a demand-oriented model of health care. Moreover, the implementation of health districts was considered by the law as a possible but not compulsory option.

3.2 THE HEALTH DISTRICT STRATEGY: TWO DIFFERENT APPROACHES

Some Brazilian states and municipalities, as well as NGOs and donors, proposed the implementation of health districts as the basic strategy to foster decentralisation and turn the principles established by the Constitution into practice.

Mendes argues that the successful implementation of the reform of the Brazilian NHS depends on a parallel action at three levels: the juridical level, where the basic norms regulating the health system are set; the institutional level of the organisation of the decentralised and unified administrative structures; and the operational level, where health services are actually organised and managed and health activities are planned, programmed, and executed.[1]

Given the relative vagueness of norms and the heterogeneity of institutional situations regarding the organisation of the health sector, the operational level becomes crucial: as a matter of fact, this is the level where concrete health actions are undertaken, their effects on the population can be assessed, and legitimacy for any given model of health care is either obtained or denied.

The strategy of attempting to decentralise health care and organise it at the district level aims to implement the principles established by the Constitution, precisely by focusing on the operational level and trying to reform the NHS in a bottom-up and 'inductive' way. The health district strategy, then, is conceived by those who propose it as the 'operational tactics to transform the NHS, in the sense of responding to the needs of the population with efficiency, effectiveness and equity'.[2]

However, two different and opposed concepts of health district are proposed to implement this strategy: the concept of health district as a social process, and the concept of health district as a bureaucratic entity.[3]

According to the latter, health districts are built up merely by delimiting a geographic, demographic and administrative space, as well as by establishing bodies for co-ordinating health activities in this space. This represents a mere process of administrative engineering: a new bureaucratic level is simply added to the existing ones, reproducing at the local level the structure of the state or municipal secretariat of health. Most important of all, the prevailing model of health care is not questioned at all: health actions are carried out in a standardised way, irrespective of the heterogeneous health needs of the population, and the approach is typically medicalised and reductionist, with little attention paid to the heterogeneous socio-economic characteristics of the population; universality of health care is accepted, but not equity – no attention is paid to the fact that a homogeneous satisfaction of health needs implies differentiated interventions, according to heterogeneous needs.[4]

In sum: the health care model which is promoted by the bureaucratic health district is typically *supply-driven*, unable to detect and act upon the real and differentiated needs of the population; with such a model, in turn, health activities are guided by mere administrative acts rather than managerial decisions.

The process approach to the implementation of health districts is led by opposite criteria. Health districts are gradually built up and their activities are implemented according to the specific and varied needs of the local population. The health district reflects its territory, which is not conceived in mere physical terms, but, rather, as the product of the interaction between different social actors, each one with his needs and demands. This territory is defined by economic, social, political, cultural and epidemiological criteria. Moreover, this is defined as 'asymmetric', as socio-economic characteristics and health needs are not distributed homogeneously in it.[5] Consequently, the health district's activities can neither be homogeneous nor standardised. Planning and programming of these activities must be guided by socio-economic and epidemiological criteria; targeting is directed towards priority problems and the specific social groups upon whom these problems are concentrated. Programming aims to mobilise resources from different sectors, in order to act upon the social and environmental determinants of ill-health. Finally, participation by the community is a prerequisite for detecting local needs and supporting decision-making.

In sum, this concept of health district promotes a *demand-driven* (or people-oriented) model of health care; needs expression is crucial for its implementation; planning and programming, in turn, require complex decision-making processes, of a managerial rather than administrative nature.

In the late 1980s those who supported the reform started implementing pilot and experimental projects, aiming to build up health districts of the process type, in different parts of Brazil. Before introducing one of these pilot experiences, however, we discuss the concepts which underlie the idea of a 'process' health district.

Health Districts, Blueprint and Process

Although we cannot mechanically find a coincidence between these models of health district and the blueprint and process approaches which we discussed in the first chapter, it is interesting to notice that elements of these approaches are actually relevant here.

In the bureaucratic health district, priorities are established at the outset by the central level, activities are highly standardised, and there is a low degree of discretion in decision-making at the local level – 'implementation' at the local level means mere execution of 'silver bullet', vertical programmes decided by the central level. These are all basic hallmarks of the blueprint approach.

The health district of the process type, on the contrary, searches for adaptation to local needs, its organisational arrangements emerge gradually from the interaction with the local environment, planning is based on social interaction and a learning process, and there is autonomy as far as decision-making at the operational level is concerned.

The concept of a process health district was influenced by the theses of Latin American authors dealing with strategic planning (among whom the most influential are Matus, Testa, and Barrenechea and Trujillo).[6] These authors tend to propose something similar to a process approach to planning. Their attempt represents a reaction against normative and technocratic models, derived from the natural sciences, like the CENDES/OPS planning method developed and widely adopted in the 1960s and early 1970s. These authors, in fact, tend to explicitly recognise:

- the political and often conflictual nature of planning;
- the need for proceeding through successive approximations in planning;
- the fact that the planner him/herself is not a neutral outsider, but, rather, an active participant in the planning process;
- the need to consider the subjective definition that the participants in a given situation give of the situation itself;
- the fact that, often, the objects of planning are uncertain, heterogeneous, and turbulent social systems, not subjected to linear causal relations, and made up of creative rather than merely reactive actors.

However, the planning models proposed by these authors are quite complex, and therefore difficult to put into operation, when they are transferred mechanically from the central level to the local one. Problems of management seem to emerge, in this respect. The emphasis given to the process aspects of planning makes the demand for specificity surrogates urgent. As a matter of fact, the need for concrete instruments to operationalise these concepts has been raised.[7] Due account was taken of this need, when projects to implement health districts of the process type started.

3.3 A PILOT HEALTH DISTRICT PROJECT IN SALVADOR, BAHIA

The state of Bahia (north-eastern Brazil), and specifically the city of Salvador, were among the sites which were chosen to implement pilot experiences of health districts. The implementation of health districts started in 1987, when eight initial districts were established in the state.

This first phase had a clear experimental character, with little or no institutional links with other reforming experiences within the health sector. The geographic and administrative boundaries of the districts were delimited, and their governing bodies were appointed (managers and executive commissions).[8]

This experiment began to be institutionalised in 1988 when 20 health districts were established in the state (eight of them in the metropolitan region of Salvador), and a specific body, the service organisation management (gerência de organização de serviços – GOS), was set within the state secretariat of health (SESAB) to manage the whole process of implementation of health districts. GOS put priority on the issue of health district management; relationships were established with PAHO and the federal University of Bahia (UFBA) to obtain support in this respect.

The idea of the health district as a flexible and adaptable institution, provided with effective decision-making capacity and open to interaction with the local population was already clear to those responsible for the process of implementation of health districts.[9]

During this phase of the process of implementation of health districts, technical co-operation activities began in Pau da Lima.

Technical Co-operation Projects in Pau da Lima

Pau da Lima was one of the eight pilot health districts of the metropolitan region of Salvador. The health district of Pau da Lima (29 sq km, 150,000 inhabitants according to 1991 estimates) is located in a suburban area of the city of Salvador (2.3 million inhabitants). Its name comes from the largest of the ten neighbourhoods which make up the district.

Pau da Lima is located in the area which represented in the 1980s, and still represents nowadays, the main vector of expansion of the city. Therefore it experienced, in the last decade, an impressive growth – its population doubled in the period 1980–91, mainly due to migration from both the interior of the state and other poor areas of the city. This growth occurred in a spontaneous and disorganised way: the process of urbanisation was very uneven, as low-to-middle-class developments constructed by the government and provided with minimum infrastructure grew side by side with illegal slums (*favelas*); these, in turn, are internally differentiated according to their age – older *favelas* tend to have better housing and infrastructure conditions than have recent ones. The health district, then, presents a high degree of internal heterogeneity – nevertheless, the picture for the area as a whole is characterised by poverty, high illiteracy, precarious infrastructure and environmental conditions.

As a consequence of this picture, the epidemiological profile of the population presented in 1988 a high frequency of diseases related to poverty and poor housing and environmental conditions, such as respiratory diseases (18.2 per cent of all the detected diseases), skin problems (16.5 per cent), intestinal problems (10.8 per cent – one-third of which were diarrhoeal problems), accidents and external causes (7.7 per cent).[10]

In 1989 the health district of Pau da Lima contained nine health centres, five of which were run by the state secretariat of health, three by the municipal secretariat of health, and one by a local philanthropic association. Most of these centres were in very bad condition, poorly equipped and understaffed. Some private clinics were present in the health district too. The health district management team was initially made up of five professionals.

At the time it was established, the health district of Pau da Lima did not go much beyond the formal blueprint, with little or no capacity to evolve towards a fully functioning, demand-oriented health district. Therefore, in 1988 it was chosen by the state secretariat of health and by an Italian non-governmental organisation (NGO) as the site for a project of technical co-operation, sponsored by the Italian government. It aimed to support a pilot health district experience which could eventually provide other health districts in the state of Bahia with an operational example. This project, with a duration of three years (March 1989–March 1992), included several activities, such as construction or repair of health infrastructures, purchase of equipment, training of health personnel, reorganisation of the health services, health education for the community, a programme of community health workers (CHWs), activities of sanitation, several research activities in the field, and institutional development. Some of these activities continued to be implemented later by the HEAP (health, environment and struggle against poverty) programme (1992–94), executed by PAHO and financed by the Italian government.

Strengthening the Health District Managerial Capacity

During the implementation of the project of Pau da Lima, the main problems and priorities for the institutional development of the health district could emerge. Consequently, some of the projects' activities were gradually reoriented in order to support a more coherent and synergistic line of intervention: activities which originally were quite dispersed were gradually integrated within a common and more focused set of objectives, guidelines and approaches. In other words, a single, 'mainstream' body of activities emerged, and the project gradually reduced its interventions to those actions which represented the key for the institutional development of the health district.

One of those keys was the development of a managerial system for the health district. This involved experimenting with, and then institutionalising operational tools to detect the local health needs, and to plan and programme appropriate actions to satisfy them. This eventually led the project staff to focus on activities related to the handling and use of information.

Clear managerial inadequacies – especially with regard to information-handling – had been pinpointed already in mid-1988, by an evaluation report of the process of implementation of health districts. The report stressed the need for an information flow to feed adequately the decision-making process, especially to detect the groups at risk and to prioritise actions towards them. The report concluded that in the districts 'health care practices are still directed almost exclusively towards the individual, clinical aspects [of ill-health], with an insufficient concern for the information which is necessary for an epidemiological approach'.[11]

Specific activities within the project were helpful to highlight the existing deficiencies at the managerial level. A consultancy undertaken by an expatriate expert in June 1989 clearly indicated the need for the project to focus its intervention on management at the local level. The main conclusions of this consultancy were the following:

- The institutional development of health districts is basically dependent on strengthening management at the local level.
- The state secretariat of health lacks effective instruments to support the development of the health district management.
- It is therefore suggested that the latter be supported through strategic and well-focused interventions, capable of multiplying their effects and of determining organisational changes within the health district.
- More specifically, it is suggested that an information system for the health district be developed: without it, in fact, the health district managerial function is blind.[12]

A consequence of this consultancy was the decision, taken by the project staff together with the co-ordination of Italian health projects in Brazil, to begin a management course for health district staff. This course took place in March 1990. The later evaluation of this course was important to reorient the project's actions further. Specifically, it was stated that:

- There is limited experience in Brazil of managing complex systems such as health districts – generally, training is focused on management of health centres only. It is crucial to develop a body of conceptual and practical *instruments* for health district management.

- It is especially necessary to develop new methodologies for the analysis of local health needs, 'aiming at building up information systems and new indicators, capable of providing health district managers with technical and administrative expertise. These systems must offer information which is relevant for decision-making, contributing, in this way, to the construction of a new "managerial culture".'[13]
- From a methodological point of view, the challenge emerges clearly 'to create a process of learning, knowledge-building and discussion about managerial problems, which comes from the practice of management itself'.[14]

These conclusions had the following effects on the project of Pau da Lima:

a) Training alone came to be seen as inadequate for strengthening the health district's managerial capacity. The project had to develop some form of 'learning by doing', together with the health district management.

b) The project and the health district management had to experiment with, develop and finally use operational tools, which had to be approached from within the daily practice of management itself.

c) More specifically, these instruments had to support the capacity of the health district management to perceive the local needs and to take complex decisions about the ways in which to satisfy them.

Health District Management in Pau da Lima: Focusing on Information-handling

In the second half of 1990, while the results of the management course were being examined, the project began a phase of adjustment of its activities. This adjustment was strongly influenced by the conclusions of the course's evaluation.

The relevance and the potential of some of the project's activities became apparent for the issues which had emerged from this evaluation. Specifically, the activities of field research, and in general of data collection, processing and use, began to play a central role in the project. These factors converged to let the aspects of information-handling emerge as crucial for the (now) explicit priority of strengthening the health district managerial capacity.

In mid-1990 an information system began to be implemented. This system was meant to be the 'nervous system' and the 'brain' of the health district of Pau da Lima, and the organisational and managerial structure of the health district would have to be shaped according to the same logic that sustained the information system.

3.4 THE EVOLUTION OF THE CONTEXT OF THE PAU DA LIMA PROJECT

During the implementation of the project of Pau da Lima the context gradually changed.

The process of decentralisation was effectively supported by the state secretariat of health (SESAB) until mid-1989, when the governor resigned in order to run as vice-president in the presidential election. As the former vice-governor took over power, the process of decentralisation of the health sector slowed down, a conflict arose between the health districts and the state's regional directories of health (DIRES), and the performance of the state public sector as a whole worsened dramatically.

An increase in overall efficiency was registered with the newly elected government (1990), coupled – however – with an attempt to centralise again some of the functions which had been previously decentralised. The role of DIRES was strengthened accordingly, and only two health districts (one of which was Pau da Lima) kept on functioning effectively.

A more effective policy in favour of the process of decentralisation was implemented, in the meantime, by the ministry of health. The health services of INAMPS (National Institute for Medical Care and Social Security) were transferred to the states and the municipalities, and guidelines were set for the gradual transfer of all the health services to the latter.

The municipality of Salvador, in turn, began to support the policy in favour of the health districts from 1990 on, first merely in opposition to the state's policy, and then (with the newly elected municipal government – end of 1992) because of a precise policy choice. Nevertheless, the institutional capacity of the municipal secretariat of health was too weak, and its financial resources too scarce, to produce any tangible results.

Thus, from mid-1989 on, an effective policy supporting the implementation of health districts did not exist in Bahia. However, this did not lead to any open conflicts between the project management and the state or municipal secretariats of health – rather, it led to some sort of 'isolation' of the Pau da Lima project.

The health district management, instead, was always a firm ally of the project management. The health district management was provided with a staff with a reasonable technical level, organised on a functional basis. This staff was gradually enlarged, and the health district management could perform all the routine functions necessary for the daily administration of the health district. This staff was quite motivated too, with regard to the aims of the reform of the NHS and the process of implementation of the health districts.

However, due to the lack of an official policy in favour of the health districts, Pau da Lima was not formalised as an autonomous administrative entity – consequently, the health district management was provided neither with budgetary autonomy, nor with resources of its own. Moreover, the health district manager had limited control over the resources of the district's health centres, as the local health services continued to depend on the state or the municipal secretariat of health. The degree of collaboration between the health district management and the health centres depended basically on the personal relationships between the health district manager and the directors of the health centres themselves.

In general, the project of Pau da Lima took place in an unfavourable context, and could count on little or no effective support from its local partners besides the health district. Other resources, both internal and external to the project, had to be employed by the project management in order to promote the institutional development of the health district. In order to obtain control over these resources for experimenting with new tools and methodologies, project management had, first, to negotiate with, and gain autonomy from, its central office in Italy; then it had to find other external supporters than the local secretariats of health, such as PAHO, the co-ordination of the Italian health projects in Brazil, and the university.

NOTES

1. E.V. Mendes, *O Sistema Unificado e Descentralizado de Saúde no Atual Contexto da Reforma Sanitária Brasileira* (Natal, Brazil: mimeo, 1987), and E.V. Mendes, *Sistemas Locais de Saúde* (Brasília: mimeo, June 1989).
2. E.V. Mendes (1989), op. cit., p. 4.
3. The description of these concepts of health districts draws on E.V. Mendes, C.F. Teixeira, E.C. Araujo and M.R.L. Cardoso, 'Distritos Sanitários: Conceitos-Chave', in E.V. Mendes (ed.), *Distrito Sanitário. O processo social de mudança das práticas sanitárias no Sistema Único de Saúde* (São Paulo e Rio de Janeiro: Hucitec/Abrasco, 1993), pp. 159–85.
4. We could say also that a health district of the bureaucratic type does not follow the principle of 'positive discrimination'. If this principle has to be followed, then more resources must be concentrated where the need is greatest, in order to try to reverse, to some extent, the situation of 'negative discrimination' of those groups which have a limited access to social services, job opportunities, basic infrastuctures and so on.
5. E.V. Mendes *et al.* (1993), op. cit., p. 167.

6. For a good review of these theses see A.H. Chorny, 'El Enfoque Estratégico para el Desarrollo de Recursos Humanos', *Educ Med Salud*, 24, 1, (1990), pp. 27–51.
7. See PAHO, *Administración Estratégica Local. Una propuesta para la discusión (versión preliminar)* (Washington, DC: PAHO, 1991).
8. The health district executive commission (*comissão executiva do distrito sanitário* – CEDS) was made up of one representative of every health centre of the district, one representative of every health service supplier present in the district (National Institute for Medical Assistance and Social Security, ministry of health, state and municipal secretariats of health, contracted philanthropic and private entities), and the health district manager.
9. E.C de Araujo and C.F. Teixeira, *Distritalização do Setor Saúde na Bahia. Momentos, Problemas e Perspectivas* (Salvador, Brazil: paper for the Italo-Brazilian meeting on NHS reform, May 1989).
10. These data, taken from a study conducted by the health district of Pau da Lima, refer to a classification of those seeking medical care at the district's health centres. Therefore, they express the epidemiological profile of those people who actually have access to these health services, rather than the epidemiological profile of the district's population as a whole. See R. Rego, E. de Souza, R. Tasca, R.V. Fernandes, *Morbidade na demanda às unidades da rede básica no Distrito Sanitário de Pau da Lima* (Salvador, Brazil: mimeo, 1989).
11. SESAB, *Elementos para o Desenho da Estratégia de Implantação dos Distritos Sanitários* (Salvador, Brazil: mimeo, July 1988), p. 14. Similar inadequacies were found in most of the pilot health districts in the whole of Brazil, as various comprehensive reports showed. The most common problems were associated both with the low managerial capacity of the human resources available at the local level, and to the lack of effective, institutional channels for social participation and the expression of needs. See ABRASCO, *A Experiência SUDS e os Desafios Atuais da Reforma Sanitária* (Rio de Janeiro: ABRASCO, 1989). Deficiencies in information-handling for demand expression and decision-making were stressed in a study which compared nine case-studies of health districts. The study argued that health care kept on being provided through normative, vertical programmes, irrespective of the heterogeneity of local needs: 'in all the cases which have been analysed, the health services' reorganisation moves from the supply [...] the inclusion in the planning process of the needs of the population has been characterised by several methodological and technical-operational difficulties'. C.M. de Almeida, *Os Atalhos da Mudança na Saúde no Brasil. Serviços em Nível Local: Nove Estudos de Caso – Uma Análise Comparativa* (Rio de Janeiro: PAHO/WHO, 1989), p. 110.
12. E. Veronesi, *Relazione sulla missione presso la Segreteria della Sanità dello Stato di Bahia* (Rome: mimeo, 1989).
13. M.C.L. Guimarães, F. Ripa di Meana, E. Foccoli and C.F. Teixeira, *A Cooperação Italiana no Brasil e o Desenvolvimento Gerencial dos Sistemas Locais de Saúde* (São Paulo: mimeo, July 1991), p. 7.
14. Ibid.

4

Knowledge-Building in Pau da Lima: Data Collection

4.1 INTRODUCTION TO KNOWLEDGE-BUILDING

In the project of Pau da Lima different activities gradually emerged as central and were integrated with each other to form a coherent set of interventions, focused on the issue of information-handling for health district management. Among these activities, those which refer to knowledge-building were crucial. A brief description of the process of knowledge-building in Pau da Lima can be useful to introduce this chapter.

Inadequacies appeared clearly, at the beginning of the project, with regard to knowledge-building. Basic information about the health district – about the socio-economic and epidemiological characteristics of its population, and about its environmental situation – were poor and out of date. Maps were out of date too, as they referred to the 1980 situation.

The decision was thus taken to collect fresh information in the field. Methods of rapid participatory appraisal were chosen to collect data on the socio-economic and environmental situation. These research activities lasted from August to December 1989, and produced reports for each of the ten *bairros* (neighbourhoods) which make up the district. Further data processing was undertaken during the first half of 1990.

By the mid-1990s it was becoming increasingly clear, however, that the project was concentrating its efforts not on 'research' per se, but, rather, on the use of the research activities for the design and implementation of an information system, aiming to support the health district management. A computer engineer was contracted to work together with the epidemiologist and the sociologist who had been working in the project so far. In the meantime, an information flow began to be structured, from the health centres to the health district management; the information collected in this way included, on the demand side, epidemiological data from patients' records and data about the patients who had registered in the health centres, and on the supply side data about the health centres' production and productivity.

By January 1991, the whole project staff was involved on a full-time basis in the development of an information system for the health district management. Project staff levels were increased to fill in the information gaps (an architect was contracted to update the existing maps), and to digitise the data and the maps in a prototype of the computerised information system. By the end of 1991 the system was almost complete and ready to be used systematically for decision-making – even if data kept on being updated and the information system design was partially modified. With the system ready for use, however, we can consider the process of knowledge-building complete, as it produced a tool usable for decision-making.

The system in its final form includes maps associated to six data bases.

The maps are made up from the following layers:

- Boundaries of the health district
- Boundaries of the health centres' responsibility areas (HCRAs)
- Boundaries of the micro-areas
- Roads (with names and numbers)
- Streams
- Health centres, schools, local associations.

The data bases are the following:

- Main characteristics of the health centres
- Patients registered in the health centres
- Diseases of compulsory notification (transmittable diseases)
- Deaths
- Socio-economic data for the HCRAs
- Socio-economic data for the micro-areas.

The main features of the maps and the data bases are illustrated in Tables A.1 and A.2, which are displayed in the Technical Appendix A.[1]

In this chapter and in the following one we analyse the whole process of knowledge-building in Pau da Lima, from data collection to the complete implementation of the information system. We focus on the gradual transformation of information into a specificity surrogate, through the progressive increase in its manageability and precision.

In this chapter attention is concentrated specifically on the first step of the process of knowledge-building in Pau da Lima – data collection for the expression of needs. In the previous chapter we said that Pau da Lima was a pilot experience for the implementation of a health district of the process type. Health districts of the process type, we argued, are basically demand-driven; this implies that special care has to be given to the detection of the needs of the resident population. We suggest that in large and heterogeneous urban areas relevant information on the resident population's needs is better collected by means of flexible and participatory methods of investigation, based on an overall process approach.

4.2 INFORMATION-HANDLING AT THE BEGINNING OF THE PROJECT

In Pau da Lima the situation of information-handling was very poor at the beginning of the project (March 1989). Here we consider two issues which acted as useful indicators of this situation, and which were influential in determining the later evolution of knowledge-building in Pau da Lima. These issues are the following:

(a) A study on secondary data, undertaken by the health district management of Pau da Lima to single out the main socio-economic and health characteristics of the district.

(b) A descriptive study on the demand for health care in Pau da Lima, conducted by the project management and the health district management.

The First Study on the Socio-economic and Health Profile of Pau da Lima[2]

In the beginning of 1989 the health district management of Pau da Lima undertook a study on the socio-economic and health profile of the district. The study used basically secondary data – estimates based on the 1980 census for the socio-economic aspects, and data produced by the state secretariat of health (SESAB) for the epidemiological aspects.

A population of 250,000 was estimated for 1989. It was not stated how this figure had been obtained (later on, the 1991 census showed a population of 150,000). Moreover, the demographic data were grouped according to the 'information zones' which make up the district, which are the administrative units used by the census; this territorial division was useless for decision-making at the district level, as it reflected neither the existing settlements, nor the constituencies of the district's health centres.

The estimated economically active population was 23,000. With a real population of 150,000, we can calculate that the economically active population would be about 25 per cent of those aged 15–60 – which is quite a low percentage. The feeling that official data did not take account of the mass of people who work in the informal sector was confirmed by the figure for open unemployment – just 3.7 per cent.

Data about income indicated that 62 per cent of the families earned less than three minimum salaries (about 200 US$ in 1989) per month, 22 per cent between three and five minimum salaries, and 16 per cent more than five minimum salaries. In this case too, official and 'standard' classifications were of little use for targeting at the district level, as the 'poor of the poor' – those who earn one minimum salary or less – were lost within data which were too aggregated.

We can find problems with data about housing and water conditions on similar grounds – excessive and/or irrelevant aggregation of data. People who lived in 'precarious housing conditions' in 1984 were 60 per cent of the total population. But the definition of 'precarious' housing conditions was not specific enough, as it included recent as well as older *favelas*, which are quite differentiated. Therefore, existing data did not differentiate between people 'at risk' and 'not at risk' with regard to housing conditions. Similarly, 63 per cent of the households in Pau da Lima had access to water in 1984 – but the kind of access was not specified: illegal linkages to the public water system, in fact, are very common in urban peripheries, and the water they supply is often contaminated, due to deficient junctions.

In contrast, data about sanitation were reasonable, as a classification was used which distinguished between situations at risk (rudimentary pits, complete lack of sanitation) and situations not at risk (linkage with sewage, septic pits). However, these data were not up to date.

With regard to epidemiological data, the situation of existing information was still worse. Data on mortality were not provided by SESAB at a level of disaggregation lower than the municipal level. Data on transmittable diseases of compulsory notification were provided (222 notifications for the period January–June 1988), but 92 per cent of the notifications were not complete. In contrast, data about the characteristics of the health services – physical infrastructure, equipment, human resources – were quite complete. As a matter of fact, these were the only data which had been collected in the field by the health district management.

The Study on the Demand for Health Care in Pau da Lima[3]

The first step implemented by the project management to provide the health district with useful information was a descriptive study of the demand for health care in Pau da Lima. A representative, random sample (ten per cent of the universe) was chosen of the 1988 clinical records of eight out of nine of the district's health centres (one centre had collected no records so far).

The most interesting result of the study referred to the geographic distribution of patients. In fact, there was no coincidence between the percentage of residents of each *bairro* and the percentage of patients who used the services provided by the health centre which was located in the same *bairro*: for instance, 36 per cent of registered patients used the health centre of Sete de Abril, whilst just 12.5 per cent of the population resided in the *bairro* of Sete de Abril. The study argued that, apparently, people tended to use those health services which guaranteed better health care, irrespective of their location; moreover, there was no evidence of correspondence between the patterns of use of health services in a given *bairro* and the concentration of health risks in the same *bairro*.

The epidemiological profile which emerged confirmed what could have been expected in a poor area such as Pau da Lima, that is, the high incidence of acute respiratory infections, skin diseases and gastro-enteritis (data are reported in the previous chapter).

However, data collected by the health centres were very poor: 15 per cent of the records lacked the patient's diagnosis, 30 per cent his/her address, and ten per cent his/her sex or age; about 50 per cent of the records provided no indications on treatment, referrals to other services, returns for further treatments.

Conclusions for Project Management

From these studies the following conclusions were drawn:

Most information (demographic, socio-economic and environmental) was out of date. Due to the rapid growth of the area of Pau da Lima – which had mainly occurred through successive waves of immigration and the creation of spontaneous settlements and slums – existing data were likely to exclude from the official figures the poorest strata of the resident population.

More precisely, existing data were not able to detect the most vulnerable groups. These, in fact, were either forgotten (demographic data and figures on the economically active population) or masked by both excessively aggregated data (income) and wrongly aggregated data (water and housing conditions). Also the existing, administrative territorial division (information zones) was a mere statistical aggregation with no relevance for the project's purposes.

The whole system of data collection was supply-oriented (it was the consequence of a supply-oriented model of health care and tended further to reinforce it): epidemiological data expressed the ill-health conditions of those who had access to health care only; such access, in turn, was strongly influenced by the characteristics of health care supply. In particular, the geographic distribution of patients reflected the different availability and/or quality of health care in different places in the district, rather than the geographic distribution of health risks; this, in turn, should have been influenced by the heterogeneous socio-economic and environmental conditions of the district – as the diseases which showed the highest incidence in Pau da Lima are generally associated with poverty and harmful housing, water and sanitation conditions. Or, at least, this possible coincidence could not be assessed, *as the geographic distribution of different socio-economic and environmental conditions was not known.*

Moreover, the available epidemiological data were also very poor: mortality data were absent, whilst the large majority of data on diseases of compulsory notification lacked crucial information. This was a clear indication of the inefficiency of the existing procedures for data collection and transmission in the health centres as well as in the state secretariat of health (SESAB).

Finally, data collected from different and parallel information systems could not be crossed with each other. This seriously limited the analytic capacity of the health district management; for instance, there were no means of assessing the available epidemiological data, and to know *who* actually had no access to health care.

From these indications, the project management could set the following priorities with regard to information-handling:

- It was necessary to collect fresh, updated information.
- This had to be disaggregated so that the existing differences in the resident population's living and health conditions became visible, and the most vulnerable groups could be identified; this disaggregation had to produce new and relevant categories, different from the ones adopted by the public administration so far.
- More specifically, these categories had to reflect the geographic distribution of health risks – which, in turn, was mainly determined by socio-economic and environmental conditions, as the epidemiological pattern of Pau da Lima indicated.

- It was necessary to modify – standardise and simplify – the procedures of data collection and transmission in the district's health centres, in order to improve the quality and timeliness of the information.
- Finally, it had to be made possible to cross different data with each other – which implied that different data had to be set into some common frame of reference, rather than into parallel information systems.

With these indications as guidelines, several activities of data collection began in Pau da Lima. In the following sections we analyse the performance of the different methods of data collection which were used to generate the new data.

We analyse two methods of data collection:

- rapid appraisal methods, for socio-economic, environmental and demographic data and the drawing of maps;
- data flows from the health centres to the health district management, for data on the patients who registered in the health centres and on transmittable diseases of compulsory notification.

The analysis is concentrated on rapid appraisal methods – the 'bulk' of knowledge-building in Pau da Lima. We do not examine data on the health centres' characteristics, as they do not refer to clients' needs. Nor are mortality data examined here, as they were generated by a standard survey on records stored by SESAB. In contrast, we prefer to concentrate on the permanent data flow which was generated from the health centres to the health district management.

4.3 PRIMARY DATA COLLECTION[4]

In this section we describe the methods of data collection used in Pau da Lima and assess their performance, with special regard to rapid appraisal's capacity to embrace different social points of view on local needs, and to unveil with some degree of locational precision existing inequalities in local living conditions.

Rapid appraisal was used in Pau da Lima to collect relevant information about needs – about the resident's population living conditions. We intend to argue that a flexible, process approach was appropriate and even necessary to collect data about local needs.

Description of Primary Data Collection[5]

The research started with the objective of providing fresh information on the socio-economic, environmental and demographic situation of the health district. This research explicitly aimed to analyse the *geographic distribution* of different socio-economic and environmental characteristics, which could represent possible health risks for the resident population.

Initially, the *bairros* were chosen as units of analysis – that is, the research aimed to compare the situation of the *bairros* and to identify those in which specific health risks were concentrated.

It was decided to use rapid appraisal methods for reasons of time and costs, as well as due to their high participatory potential.

A questionnaire was prepared by the project staff's sociologist and two epidemiologists of the health district management. It included questions on the physical environment and the existing infrastructure, on the socio-economic situation, on health conditions and the use of local health services, and on the existing local associations and their achievements. The questionnaire was open and flexible enough to allow interviewees to express with some degree of freedom their felt needs.

Fieldwork started in mid-August 1989. It was carried out by students contracted from the local university. It was conducted according to a typical process approach: at the end of each day, data which had been collected were analysed and to some extent systematised, and decisions were taken by the research team on what information to collect the following day, where, and from what type of interviewees. Data which were being collected were referred to geographic locations on the map. In this way, an initial and still provisional 'geographic grid' was constructed, which was then used as a guide to orient further fieldwork. Then, a complete picture of each *bairro* was gradually defined by means of successive approximations.

Information was provided by key informants, that is, by people who were supposed to possess relevant knowledge about the characteristics of their community, due to the position they held within the community itself. Key informants were chosen among local leaders, doctors and nurses who worked in the area, shopkeepers and traders, teachers, as well as ordinary people. The total sample, made up of different key informants, was built up according to a 'snowball' method[6] – that is, each person who had been interviewed was asked to indicate other, potential key informants. It is clear that an accurate selection of key informants was crucial to guarantee some sort of representativeness of the sample – different types of people had to be contacted in order to obtain different points of view about a common set of local needs and problems.

The whole research process was conducted under my supervision – I was on the project's staff as manager of the 'social area'.[7]

In this way, by the end of 1989 the whole district had been covered, and standard reports were ready for each one of the *bairros*. At this stage it began to appear clearly that the *bairro* was not a meaningful unit of analysis, as it was internally too heterogeneous; therefore, no comparisons could be made between different *bairros*, nor was it possible to prioritise among them. In other words, at the end of fieldwork project management began to notice that local variability in Pau da Lima was much greater and geographically more dispersed than expected, and that categories smaller and more precise than the *bairros* had to be defined to support decision-making.

Assessment of the Performance of Rapid Appraisal Methods

The performance of rapid appraisal methods can be assessed by analysing in depth the questionnaires used during field-work. Other information has been provided by notes taken during the rapid appraisal itself.

The following dimensions of the performance of rapid appraisal methods are assessed:

- coverage, which we define as the capacity to collect data from different social points of view on local needs;
- locational precision, which we define as the capacity by interviewees to identify significant differences in living conditions within their *bairros*, and to key them to specific geographic locations.

Coverage as well as locational precision are assessed as rapid appraisal methods were chosen in order to overcome some inadequacies of existing, official data – namely, their inability both to reach the different social groups who reside in Pau da Lima, and to detect differences in their living conditions through the analysis of their geographic distribution. By assessing the performance of rapid appraisal methods in this respect, we intend to see (a) to what extent a flexible approach was necessary in Pau da Lima to 'cover' different social points of view about local needs, and (b) to what extent such an approach was capable of providing precise as well as manageable data about relevant differences in local needs – data which could begin to approximate information to a specificity surrogate (only with such data, in fact, would it be possible to define, later on in decision-making, clear targets, goals and actions).

Coverage

The assessment of coverage is focused on the key informants who were interviewed. Key informants were indicated as collectively recognised 'experts' – generally, due to the length of residence in the area and the position they held within the local social networks. These indications, however, could generally guarantee the contact with well-informed residents, but not necessarily with widely representative points of view. Therefore, in each moment of the research process, researchers had to select, among the possible key informants, those 'social types' whose opinions had not been heard so far. In other words, the selection of key informants had to be guided by a deliberate research strategy, aiming to build up gradually a wide and socially differentiated sample.

The analysis of the key informants who were interviewed, then, is helpful in elucidating this research strategy and the degree of 'social coverage' by the research itself.

Eighty-seven rapid appraisal questionnaires are analysed, in order to see what types of key informants have been contacted. Figures are available in the Technical Appendix A, Table A.3.

The analysis indicates that key informants from the community (local leaders, old residents, traders and shopkeepers) prevail over those from the institutions (teachers and personnel from the health centres). This is important, as – we remember – the research started from the awareness of the biases and incompleteness of information collected by the institutions themselves.

Moreover, local leaders are the largest group of key informants, followed by old residents. This could be interpreted as the result of a research strategy aiming to 'balance' the leaders' opinions (and possible biases) with those of ordinary people.

Therefore, we can conceptualise a research strategy that aimed to get progressively deeper into the collection and use of real grass-roots knowledge on local needs by contacting three levels of decreasingly institutionalised key informants: institutions, leaders, ordinary people. This strategy is consistent with the aims of the research to cover different 'social' points of view about local needs.

As far as coverage is concerned, we must stress the importance of an open and flexible research design, which did not select interviewees at the outset, but rather identified them gradually, according to the information needs which emerged during the research process itself. However, we must stress the importance of a deliberate research strategy and of systematic procedures in the field, based on the ongoing analysis of incoming data; this allowed the research team to manage appropriately the research process in the field, especially with regard to the selection of the key informants who were needed at any given time of the research process itself.[8]

Locational precision

In the assessment of the locational precision of rapid appraisal methods we test the respondents' capacity to 'key' precisely the information they provided to specific geographic locations within their *bairros*. The rapid appraisal questionnaires of two *bairros* are analysed, and each answer is classified according to explicit territorial references which can be found in the text. Data, together with a description of the techniques used to classify them, can be found in the Technical Appendix A (Table A.4).

Our analysis indicates a medium performance in terms of locational precision. In both *bairros,* slightly less than half of the answers are locationally precise – that is, the majority of the answers cannot reveal relevant differences in local living conditions. It seems that key informants are unlikely to be capable of providing meaningful differentiated information about certain local characteristics, such as the income distribution, education, the use of health facilities, and the most frequent diseases. For these items, investigation by secondary (official) sources, or sound research techniques would be more appropriate – although their limitations in terms of time and cost should always be considered cautiously. In contrast, visible characteristics of the location, such as sanitation, housing conditions, and availability of water, are likely to be more easily distinguished by key informants. These items refer to specific and visible aspects of poverty. We can therefore argue that key informants in an urban, heterogeneous area such as Pau da Lima tend to provide more accurate information on visible aspects of poverty. Data which seem to support such a hypothesis are also available in the Technical Appendix A.

We analysed also the type of answers most frequently provided by different types of informants (see Technical Appendix A). We saw that the personnel from the health centres tend to provide differentiated information about the *bairro* as a whole, whereas old residents tend to provide very accurate information about the portion of the *bairro* where they live. This seems to indicate the appropriateness of a research strategy that contacted informants from institutions first, for a general overview of the *bairro* (probably made possible by the frequent contacts that these people have with residents from the whole *bairro* itself), and then informants from the community, for insights about specific sub-areas.

In sum, the previous analysis seems to indicate that only to a certain extent (that is, for some items only) were key informants capable of providing locationally precise information on local living conditions. Key informants were capable of providing *indications* about relevant differences in living conditions – not a precise and neat picture of them. These indications were useful in building up and gradually filling in a geographic grid. However, this grid represented just a provisional hypothesis of territorial division – a preliminary approximation to reality. Local knowledge was valuable in providing these indications – that is, in taking a first step towards precise information on local living conditions – but this was not enough, as neither exact, nor manageable categories were made available to decision-makers.

In this respect, the use of a geographic grid to interpret and classify information on the basis of its territorial reference was necessary but not sufficient to transform the information itself into a specificity surrogate. Other tools and a different approach, as we shall see in the next chapter, had to be used.

Initial Conclusions on Primary Data Collection

Initial deficiencies in information-handling were basically overcome. Different methods were used to collect socio-economic, environmental and demographic data. From a methodological point of view all these methods were unorthodox ('quick and dirty'), and relied basically on a process approach.

Notwithstanding some limits in terms of locational precision, rapid appraisal methods provided useful indications about relevant differences in local living conditions, at least for some local characteristics. Moreover, information covered a wide range of social points of view on local needs.

A flexible research design was important in contacting socially differentiated key informants. A deliberate research strategy together with systematic procedures were important in selecting the 'right' informant at the 'right' time. Moreover, a geographic grid was helpful in interpreting and classifying provisionally the incoming information, and in directing the research strategy itself.

A systematic research strategy aiming to contact informants who were progressively 'less institutionalised' was crucial, as each level or type of informants could provide different but equally useful types of information. The 'institutional' informants are more likely to generalise (or talk about averages), or to provide information on a number of different localised areas – their awareness, in fact, is that of someone with more overview and comparative capacity. In contrast, the personal knowledge of the 'less institutionalised' informants is usually geographically more limited (but also richer and more accurate), as their 'living space' is smaller – they are, consequently, more likely to refer to localised areas, and specifically to the one they know. However, both types of knowledge were useful in Pau da Lima. Through an appropriate selection of informants, different data were mutually complemented and completed – relevant data on different local areas, provided by different informants, could be gradually assembled to build up a picture of the health district as a whole. The possibility of assembling different data from different key informants by means of a geographic grid provided researchers with preliminary indications about the spatial distribution of living conditions and needs.

We must stress also that the satisfactory performance of data collection was due to the motivation and commitment of the fieldwork team, who was provided with appropriate incentives. The fieldworkers performed satisfactorily due to appropriate recruitment, training, and supervision during fieldwork. Moreover, they were directly contracted by the project, and made accountable to it. Open discussions were crucial in building up consensus about objectives and means and in increasing the degree of motivation of the staff.

4.4 SECONDARY DATA COLLECTION

Secondary data are those data which were collected from the health centres, and which referred to the demand for health care of the population of Pau da Lima.

For the new information system which had to be implemented in Pau da Lima, it had to be made clear that data on the demand for health care did not necessarily reflect the health needs of the resident population as a whole. On the contrary, they reflected the health needs of those who had access to health care only, and who were just a part of the whole resident population. Consequently, it became crucial to control the biases of data on the demand for health care. For that, two different sets of data had to be used, with different purposes.

Data on the living conditions of the population should provide indications about the *health needs* of the resident population. These data were necessary to take strategic decisions about priority target groups – to concentrate resources where the need was greatest, and to programme a set of actions most of which would be executed outside the health centres (educational activities, screening of subjects at risk, home visits, and so on), as well as in collaboration with sectors other than health. We saw that these data were collected in the field by means of rapid appraisal methods.

In contrast, data on the demand for health care were necessary to take administrative decisions about the functioning of the health centres (allocation of human resources, purchase of equipment, supply of drugs and so on). These data had to be collected inside the health centres.

Data collected inside the health centres presented serious deficiencies. Activities were implemented by the project staff to improve the procedures for data collection and transmission in the health centres of Pau da Lima.

Each health centre of the district had its own procedures of data collection, so that no standardisation was possible within the existing procedures. Moreover, data were collected irregularly, and most forms were not complete. As a general practitioner of the health district staff put it, 'doctors will never fill in the existing forms, nor are the clerks skilled enough to do that'.[9] Existing forms and procedures had to be simplified, then.

Moreover, the possibility had to be provided of crossing data on the demand for health care with data on living conditions. Such a comparison should allow the health district management to control the biases of the former, by assessing for what part of the population these were valid, and estimating the existing gap between the needs which were expressed through the access to the health centre, and the health needs which were not visible. This comparison could be made possible through the reference of both sets of data to a common geographic overlay.

Project management decided, then, to collect two basic sets of data inside the health centres:

- Data on the characteristics of that part of the population who used the health services, in order to know who actually had access to the latter and who had not (data on the registered population in the health centres).
- Data about the epidemiological characteristics of this population (transmittable diseases of compulsory notification).

Description of Secondary Data Collection[10]

Simplified forms and procedures were designed and implemented in order to collect data from the health centres. Most of the socio-economic questions included in family forms which patients had to fill in were avoided. The distribution of relevant data in the health district territory was already known through the rapid appraisal survey, and it *would be sufficient to know the patient's address to know, with reasonable approximation, his or her living conditions too.* The reference of the individual patient to a portion of the territory whose characteristics were known allowed a crucial simplification in data collection.[11]

Data on the patients who registered in the health centres were collected by means of a simple registration form. Clerks in the health centres were trained, and a manual with detailed instructions was distributed to them. Data from the registration forms were digitised into a data base.

Medical data for each patient were collected by the attending doctor, and copied in the patient's clinical record. When a transmittable disease was detected by the doctor, its occurrence was reported in a weekly bulletin of compulsory notification, which was regularly sent to the health district unit of epidemiological surveillance, and digitised into a data base.

Assessment of the Performance of Secondary Data Collection

Data on registered patients began to be collected in one of the health centres of the *bairro* of Castelo Branco (CSU Castelo Branco), and then the same procedures were gradually implemented in all the district's health centres.

After the first 1,500 patients were registered in the Castelo Branco health centre, a check was made on the quality of data collected so far. The results were quite disappointing: notwithstanding training and the new and simpler forms and procedures, 50 per cent of forms were found with some mistakes in their data – most often, the patient's registration number. Mistakes were basically attributable to clerks, who had filled in the forms incorrectly, or to digitisers, who had introduced wrong data into the data base.

The existing registration forms were enlarged – semi-literate clerks had complained about the difficulty of writing in small spaces. Moreover, the clerk at the health district headquarters who was already in charge of checking the digitised data was taught to produce data base reports. These reports, which were produced regularly for each new batch of data, were returned to the health centre clerks, and had to be compared by them with the original patients' forms stored in the health centre and mistakes corrected. Moreover, the computer was programmed so that the registration number of each patient was digitised automatically.

These simple modifications in the procedures of data collection led to a significant improvement in the quality of data. Improvements were possible because: (a) mistakes could be immediately detected, together with their sources – clear and simple procedures made the causes of low performance immediately traceable; and (b) operators received feedback on the results of their activities, and could correct mistakes which had been made.

With regard to the collection of data on diseases of compulsory notification, a positive trend was registered as a result of the new procedures. According to an assessment undertaken by the health district management,[12] complete notifications were 70 per cent or more of all notifications in the health centres of CSU Castelo Branco, Dom Avelar and Nova Brasília; the same figure was between 50 and 70 per cent in the health centre of Cana Brava and in the philanthropic health centre of Mansão do Caminho, and below 30 per cent in the health centres of Novo Marotinho, UMO Castelo Branco and UMO Pau da Lima, which, however, had started to collect data later than the other centres. Previously, 92 per cent of all notifications had been registered as not complete.

Initial Conclusions on Secondary Data Collection

After some initial difficulties, data on patients registered in the health centres were collected regularly and accurately. The performance of data on diseases of compulsory notification was satisfactory too.

Simplified forms and standard, clear procedures were responsible for the good performance of secondary data collection. This was especially the case for data on patients who registered in the health centres, for which very detailed instructions, written in a 'Taylorist' style, were provided to clerks. This clear division and organisation of work improved the capacity to trace clearly the causes of an initially low performance, to provide supervision and steps for adjustment, and to provide operators with feedback about their job performance.

The adequate training of the health centres' clerks was also responsible for the good performance of secondary data collection. As for primary data collection, open discussions between the project's staff and the clerks made clear what benefits the latter would receive from following properly the new procedures of data collection.

4.5 DISCUSSION: FLEXIBILITY AND SPECIFICITY IN NEEDS EXPRESSION

In Pau da Lima the whole process of knowledge-building started from the existence of specific information gaps and from perceived problems about information-handling in general. Most available data were out of date; some social groups were forgotten or masked by these data, which were either too aggregated or grouped in a useless way; the administrative categories used to divide the district's territory were equally useless for the project's purposes; data collected by the health centres were incomplete and not standardised; and finally, different data could not be crossed with each other.

These problems were to some extent overcome. Rapid appraisal methods and simplified forms and procedures were used to improve data collection. Both primary and secondary data collection performed satisfactorily. However, the underlying mechanisms were quite different.

Blueprint and Process: Secondary and Primary Data Collection

Secondary data collection can be seen as an inherently highly-specific activity, for which flexibility was not needed at all – a typical blueprint activity. Simplified forms, standard procedures and detailed instructions were the devices used to improve data collection. Activities were broken down into smaller components and executed with little discretion by unskilled operators. Some supervision was obviously needed, but without constant and daily decisions as in primary data collection. A low performance was immediately recognised, its causes were easily traced, and readjustments had to be made with a much lower frequency than in primary data collection.

The same procedures could not be used to collect data on local living conditions and needs. The collection of primary data was a typical activity of the process type, conducted by means of successive approximations. For rapid appraisal methods precise rules could not be set, and skilled fieldworkers had to be allowed some degree of discretion and to be provided with technical support.

An overall process approach was necessary to collect meaningful data on local needs – that is, *to deal with people* who had to express their needs. Rapid appraisal methods were used because of the lack of resources (time and money). But other advantages of these methods emerged, such as a participatory potential based on social interaction between the researchers and the community, the ability to cover a wide range of social points of view, and the capacity to pick up relevant local knowledge. All these positive features were made possible by the flexible nature of rapid appraisal methods.

Flexibility and Rapid Appraisal

In people-oriented activities, knowledge-building needs flexibility. It must be based on social interaction and incrementalism, if beneficiaries are to be allowed to express their needs.

In Pau da Lima, the openness of rapid appraisal questionnaires encouraged the spontaneity of key informants and enhanced the interaction between fieldworkers and members of the community. The subjectivity of each informant could be expressed and adequately considered in data collection.

It is important to handle appropriately the subjectivity of the informants, as the definition itself of problems and needs implies a subjective dimension and depends on the individual experience – especially when issues related to health and disease are considered.[13] Open questions and a real dialogue between researchers and informants are crucial conditions for subjectivity to be expressed. The researcher must perform a facilitating role if the community members are to contribute to the collective knowledge of the system.[14]

However, a picture based on different subjectivities can be made objective – that is, reliable and complete – only if a wide and differentiated spectrum of informants is contacted. Key informants can be a major tool in rapid appraisal methods; nevertheless, it is fundamental to cross-check the different indications provided by them, as often 'key informants tend to be the better off, the better educated, and the more powerful'.[15] Potential biases can be controlled by contacting different social types of key informants.

In Pau da Lima, an open and flexible research design was crucial to the gradual construction of a wide and socially differentiated sample, and to the articulation of different perspectives with each other. Such a design was successful in picking up some knots of the networks of reciprocal exchange of information at the community level.[16] The 'snowball' method of sample construction worked through indications which key informants provided about other, potential key informants; all key informants were likely to participate in common networks of communication and exchange. The process of sample construction, therefore, followed these networks. A pre-established and fixed sample could never have done it.

These networks are typically local: physical proximity is essential for their existence and working.[17] The information exchanged in small-scale local areas among the members of these networks is economically valuable, as it deals with basic needs and the ways in which to satisfy them[18] – the issues in which the whole process of data collection in Pau da Lima was most interested. Within these local contexts of social interaction, a common body of knowledge is shaped largely by means of face-to-face, oral interactions.

The importance of well-localised knowledge by the community of Pau da Lima was previously stressed – we saw that the 'less institutionalised' key informants tended to provide data which were relevant insofar as they were keyed to small local areas. Moreover, open and flexible rapid appraisal methods, based mainly on oral interaction with community members, were crucial in gaining access to relevant knowledge on the basic needs of the marginalised social groups of Pau da Lima.

We argue, then, that flexible and participatory methods of data collection can be very effective in the collection of data on needs in poor urban areas. In these areas the access to the market is limited and the action of the state is virtually absent, and the actual living conditions of the resident population are mainly the product of survival strategies based on self-provision or the reciprocal exchange of goods and services aimed at satisfying subsistence needs. These strategies, which are strongly influenced by the subjectivity of the actors, cannot be interpreted by means of 'objective' research methods alone. In contrast, they are better understood when also hermeneutic methods of data collection, based on social interaction, are used.[19]

Data Collection and Project Management

In both primary and secondary data collection, traditional managerial tools such as training and supervision were important in increasing the degree of motivation of the staff. However, the adoption of an open, interactive and collaborative managerial style was equally important in this respect. In particular, the interaction between the project management and its local partners was focused on *how* to develop the methods and instruments of information-handling, so that they could 'fit in' with the needs and capacities of the available human resources. In this way, these methods and instruments could be readjusted – more categorically for the blueprint activities, and more gradually for the process ones. In this respect, the experimental and incremental way in which these methods and instruments were implemented was crucial for motivating their users. Through experimentation, gradualism and interaction, the participants were made aware of why and how they had to execute certain activities, hence increasing their degree of motivation and commitment and, in the end, improving their performance.

4.6 CONCLUSIONS

The methods of data collection used in Pau da Lima worked reasonably well. Different devices, of the process and the blueprint type respectively, had to be used, due to the varying nature of the information to be collected and, consequently, of the activities to be performed.

The collection of data on needs was a typical activity of the process type. It was implemented according to criteria of flexibility. This resulted in the actual collection of relevant information.

However, the adoption of an overall process approach, even if necessary in the first stage of knowledge-building, provided just an initial approximation to the construction of an exact picture of differences in local living conditions. As we shall see in the next chapter, a more balanced approach between process and blueprint was necessary in the following step of knowledge-building in Pau da Lima, in order to approximate the information so far collected to a specificity surrogate.

NOTES

1. In order to make the central argumentation of the present study clearer, from this chapter onwards some tables, maps, and the description of the methodologies adopted have been included in a Technical Appendix. Its reading is suggested for those who might be interested in replicating the approach originally developed in Pau da Lima.
2. R. V. Fernandes, *Estudo sobre o perfil sócio-económico e de saúde do Distrito Sanitário Pau da Lima* (Salvador, Brazil: mimeo, 1989).
3. R. Rego, E. de Souza, R. Tasca and R.V. Fernandes, *Morbidade na demanda às unidades da rede básica no Distrito Sanitário de Pau da Lima* (Salvador, Brazil: mimeo, 1989).

4. We consider as 'primary' data only the fresh information which has been generated in the field and from direct contact with the local population. All other data are considered as 'secondary'.
5. For more technical details on the procedures for the collection of primary data, see the Technical Appendix A.
6. G. Rose, *Deciphering Sociological Research* (London: Macmillan, 1982), p. 50.
7. For more technical information on the use of rapid appraisal methods in health districts in Brazil, see F. Notarbartolo di Villarosa, R. Tasca and R.V. Fernandes, 'Análise da Situação Sócio-sanitária, Microlocalização e Participação no Distrito Sanitário de Pau da Lima', *Revista Baiana de Saúde Pública*, 17, 1–4 (1990), pp. 7–14, and F. Notarbartolo di Villarosa, *A Estimativa Rápida e a Divisão do Território no Distrito Sanitário. Manual de Instruções* (Brasília: PAHO, Brazilian Office, Série Desenvolvimento de Serviços de Saúde N°11, 1993). For a good review of the applications of rapid assessment procedures in public health in general, see L. Manderson and P. Aaby, 'An Epidemic in the Field? Rapid Assessment Procedures and Health Research', *Social Science and Medicine*, 35, 7 (1992), pp. 839–50.
8. Several similarities exist between the rapid appraisal methods used in Pau da Lima and the more general methodology of qualitative case-studies. Case-studies are typically applied to the investigation of organisations or communities; informants are intentionally selected; and a mixture of methods tends to be used. See D.J. Casley and D.A. Lury, *Data Collection in Developing Countries* (Oxford: Clarendon Press, 1987), pp. 64–5. According to Rose, qualitative fieldwork evolves over time – it is basically a process. It tends to adopt a blend of theoretical and accidental sampling, as 'samples are not selected in advance, and decisions on what to do next are made as part of the on-going field-work process' (G. Rose (1982), op. cit., p. 120). Data analysis also is a cyclical, cumulative process, which aims at a 'progressive refinement or revision of results until they are consistent with the data' (G. Rose, op.cit., p. 124), searching for consciously tentative patterns. In sum, then, qualitative methods (and rapid appraisal methods among them) cannot be tightly structured in advance; on the contrary, they must be based on an open and flexible design (especially with regard to sampling), and must proceed by means of successive approximations. The fluid process of fieldwork, however, must be guided by a rigorous and systematic strategy. This, according to Casley and Lury, implies a complete dependence on the investigators' ability, experience, and ingenuity – that is, on professionalism (D.J. Casley and D.A. Lury (1987), op. cit., p. 65). Professionalism seems to be required in rapid appraisal, with regard to the need for a close, technical supervision of field-work.
9. Personal statement by a health district doctor, pronounced during a meeting of the district's executive commission, July 1989.
10. For more information on the procedures used to collect secondary data, see the Technical Appendix A.
11. Obviously, this assumption is valid just insofar as the 'portion of the territory' to which the individual patient is referred is relatively homogeneous with regard to its socioeconomic and environmental characteristics. For a detailed

discussion of this issue, see the next chapter.

12. Gerência Distrito Sanitário Pau da Lima, *Boletim Epidemiológico Janeiro à Junho 1993* (Salvador, Brazil: mimeo, 1991).
13. See J.D. Mayer, 'Challenges to Understanding Spatial Patterns of Disease: Philosophical Alternatives to Logical Positivism', *Social Science and Medicine*, 35, 4 (1992), p. 582. This was confirmed by many interviews in Pau da Lima, where it appeared clearly that different social groups had different 'thresholds' for dividing the state of health from the state of disease. This led the poorest and more marginalised people to search for medical care only when the disease had reached an advanced state. I reached similar conclusions in a study on the access to health care services by street children in Salvador, Bahia. See F. Notarbartolo di Villarosa and A. Bunschaft, 'Bambini di strada e accesso ai servizi socio-sanitari a Salvador de Bahia, Brasile', *Percorsi di Integrazione*, 2, 1 (1993), pp. 23–30.
14. D.C. Korten, 'The Management of Social Transformation', *Public Administration Review*, 41, (Nov.–Dec. 1981), p. 613.
15. R. Chambers, 'Rapid Rural Appraisal: Rationale and Repertoire', *Public Administration and Development*, 1 (1981), p. 102.
16. Lomnitz Adler makes a comprehensive analysis of these networks for the shanty towns of Mexico. See L. Lomnitz Adler, *Networks and Marginality. Life in a Mexican Shantytown* (New York, San Francisco and London: Academic Press, 1982) pp. 131-157. Besides information, also goods and services are usually exchanged in these networks.
17. L. Lomnitz Adler (1982), op. cit., p. 134.
18. L. Lomnitz Adler (1982), op. cit., p. 132.
19. Some studies in urban sociology provide interesting insights on this issue. According to Pahl, the local survival strategies (or household work strategies) are not mechanistically determined by the structural characteristics of the context, as they are deeply influenced by the specific culture of the local milieu. Consequently, a well-balanced perspective in terms of local political economy and micro-cultural styles is necessary to an understanding of a given locality. See R.E. Pahl, 'The Restructuring of Capital, the Local Political Economy and Household Work Strategies', in D. Gregory and J. Urry (eds), *Social Relations and Spatial Structures* (London: MacMillan, 1984), pp. 253–4. Similarly, Dickens distinguishes between 'locales' (given spaces allocated to certain uses) and 'localities' (local social systems). The perspective of the 'locality' – of the way in which people interact in small local contexts – is crucial to understanding the social identities of people and the way they live outside the sphere of the market. See P. Dickens, *Urban Sociology. Society, Locality and Nature* (Hemel Hempstead, Hertfordshire: Harvester Wheatsheaf, 1990).

5

Knowledge-Building in Pau da Lima: Data Processing

5.1 INTRODUCTION TO DATA PROCESSING

Data processing was the second stage in knowledge-building in Pau da Lima. Relevant data were collected through rapid appraisal methods. However, these data still had to be made manageable for analytic use and decision-making. They had to be simplified and made comparable with each other.

In sum, problems of *systematisation*, *standardisation* and *manageability* of information had to be solved.

Through systematisation and standardisation, information had to be turned into a specificity surrogate. This could be achieved by increasing its capacity to express in a clear, manageable and precise way relevant differences in local living conditions, thus improving its effectiveness in supporting decision-making. More elements from the blueprint approach were used to treat information than in data collection. Information was subjected to a more intensive and systematic analytic treatment. Moreover, data were computerised.

5.2 PRIMARY DATA PROCESSING

Data collected by means of rapid appraisal methods were systematised into reports for each *bairro*, which described the main characteristics and internal differences of the latter. However, reports were quite descriptive, and therefore unsuitable for immediate use for analytic purposes. Moreover, according to the reports each *bairro* was showing an internal variability in living conditions which was much higher than expected.

The project management concluded that, because of this internal heterogeneity, the *bairros* were neither precise nor manageable categories. If the *bairros* had been chosen as units of analysis, then differences in living conditions would have been masked by aggregated data. Due to the internal heterogeneity in living conditions, there was no point in comparing whole *bairros* with each other, as it was impossible to take decisions about the degree of priority to be assigned to each *bairro*. Consequently, it was decided to subject the available information to a further analytic treatment, in order to increase its degree of precision as well as manageability. Data were treated in order to be systematised into categories which reflected existing differences in a clear-cut as well as manageable way.

Description of Primary Data Processing

The differences in living conditions identified within each *bairro* coincided with different types of human settlements. Provisionally, these settlements were grouped into three types, namely buildings planned and constructed by the government, spontaneous but legal settlements, and spontaneous and illegal settlements or slums.

This initial attempt made the project management aware of the need and opportunity to construct clear-cut territorial categories, smaller than the *bairros*, which could reflect the different living conditions existing within the *bairros* themselves. For this, information contained in the reports had to be systematised and standardised in a clearer and simpler format.

Systematisation

Rapid appraisal data were analysed again, and were grouped according to their territorial references within each *bairro*. Simple tables of comparison were prepared to analyse the spatial distribution of data and to systematise the available information according to a still provisional territorial division. This was based on geographic categories which were smaller than the *bairros*, and which were called micro-areas. These were roughly equivalent to the human settlements identified within each *bairro*.

The columns of the tables referred to the provisional micro-areas, while the different items considered in the reports, such as housing, water and sanitation conditions, income levels, and so on, were placed in the rows.

Subsequently, the tables' columns were carefully analysed to assess the internal homogeneity of each micro-area; the rows were analysed to assess the differences for each item between the micro-areas. When the differences *internal* to each micro-area turned out to be smaller than the differences *between* micro-areas, the initial territorial division was confirmed; otherwise, this division was readjusted in a more convincing manner. This process was conducted in a very systematic way – each bit of information was analysed with care and methodically cross-checked with the others. Through this regular comparison, data could be rearranged into more precise and definite categories.

In this way, the entire territory of the district could be divided into micro-areas, for which simple and synthetic tables containing the most relevant information were available (an example is provided in Table B.2 in the Technical Appendix B). The precise boundaries of the micro-areas were drawn on the map of the district so that information could be keyed to clear-cut geographic locations.

Standardisation

Most data contained in the tables were qualitative, and therefore not directly comparable. Comparisons between single items or micro-areas as a whole still required a considerable interpretative effort. Consequently, quantitative scores were attributed to qualitative data in the micro-areas' tables, so as to order different levels of living conditions (and, by inference, of health risk) into a rank.

Scores were attributed in a very simple way. For each item, the different situations existing in the health district were listed and then ranked. Subsequently, these different situations were grouped so as to create four types for each item, which were given a score between one (minimum risk) and four (maximum risk). Systematic procedures were needed to list, compare and rank the different situations. A thorough analysis based on the technical assessment of different types of risk was essential for that. A concrete example of this procedure is provided in the Technical Appendix B.

With the systematisation of information into tables and its standardisation through the attribution of scores, primary data processing was complete, and data collected through rapid appraisal methods were made suitable for direct and simple analytic use. In their final form, these data were disaggregated at the level of micro-areas, systematised into simple, descriptive tables, and standardised through the attribution of scores.

Assessment of Primary Data Processing

We proceed now to the assessment of the reliability of data collected through rapid appraisal methods and of the validity of the territorial division into micro-areas.

We selected three micro-areas, as representative of types of settlement in Pau da Lima. Then we selected for analysis the main indicators of living conditions from the micro-areas' tables. Finally we compared these data (which had been collected through rapid appraisal methods) with data obtained by means of an orthodox household survey in the field, with a statistically representative sample and a structured questionnaire. This survey was directed by the project staff and consultants, as part of a study of informal survival strategies in Pau da Lima.[1]

Figures are shown and discussed in the Technical Appendix B (Tables B.1 and B.2).

Reliability

The reliability of the tables for the micro-areas is tested by comparing the rapid appraisal data with the household survey data. The closer the coincidence between these data, the higher the reliability of the tables.

Rapid appraisal data on housing conditions, water and jobs (at least with regard to the basic distinction between formal and informal workers) perform well in terms of reliability. Data on sanitation are reliable too, and rapid appraisal methods are more effective than survey methods in detecting risks for the micro-area as a whole, rather than for the individual households. Income data, in contrast, seem to be unsuitable for collection through rapid appraisal methods.

Validity

Categories are considered as valid insofar as they effectively reflect what they are meant to measure. In Pau da Lima, data were grouped into categories which we called micro-areas, in order to make visible the existing differences in local living conditions. Then, the micro-areas are valid categories only if they effectively indicate such differences. The validity of the micro-areas can be tested by analysing if they are internally homogeneous and externally differentiated – that is, if the differences in living conditions within the micro-areas themselves are smaller than the same differences between different micro-areas.

The test is made by using household survey data as a reference. We examine if differences in living conditions are expressed in similar ways in both rapid appraisal and survey data.

Household survey data confirm immediately those rapid appraisal data which refer to water, housing, and – at least partially – jobs. For these items, significant differences coincide among the micro-areas considered. Household survey data show a certain varability internal to each micro-area for the items of sanitation and income. Nevertheless, in this case, also, a closer analysis indicates that the differences internal to each micro-area are less remarkable than those among the micro-areas themselves.

We previously saw that rapid appraisal data about income are hardly reliable. Now we can see that these data, although unreliable in terms of absolute values, are reliable in terms of ranking. The income level of each micro-area is incorrect, but the ranking of the micro-areas in terms of income is right. This suggests that key informants are not reliable with regard to absolute income levels, but they are capable of indicating actual differences in this respect: they are capable of saying who earns more and – most important of all – they identify with certainty who earns less, which is what really matters for our purposes.

The test indicates that the micro-areas are relatively homogeneous categories, which actually express relevant differences in local living conditions. The existing differences internal to each micro-area are less relevant than the differences among the micro-areas themselves – the latter rather than the former indicate a threshold in terms of intensity of risk.

The differences in living conditions expressed by the territorial division into micro-areas are relevant from an operational point of view – that is, from the point of view of management which has to detect the most vulnerable social groups, and to locate them in well-delimited areas. Both rapid appraisal and household survey data, in fact, indicate that, notwithstanding its relative internal differentiation, one micro-area presents an overall higher level of risk than the other two micro-areas considered, and consequently that it would be correct to prioritise it as a possible target.

De Kadt and Tasca elaborate a distinction between the process of identifying people at risk, and the operational detection and 'marking out' of those who should be targeted by the health services.[2] The epidemiological risk approach based on screening procedures focused on individual characteristics, is capable of identifying categories of people at risk (for instance female-headed households), but may run into problems with the actual 'marking out' of these categories in the field, especially when the resources for implementing the process of screening are limited. The opposite approach, focused on social determinants of health and ill-health, is called the 'life chances approach'. The chance to satisfy health needs is seen as a part of wider life chances – which ultimately derive from a person's position in the social structure.

Different life-chances influence different probabilities of getting sick, and of being picked up as 'at risk' by the screening activities. With scarce resources, and with an unequal and generally scarce access to health care, the risk approach is likely to make mistakes of exclusion (of subjects at risk) and inclusion (of subjects not at risk).[3] Screening, and then targeting according to life chances, is more efficient, effective and equitable. However, the authors correctly argue that concepts like 'health chances', or 'life chances' are too general to be implemented in practice. Therefore, the 'life-chances' approach might run into the typical problems of people-oriented activities – problems of management, implementation, and lack of specificity. The risk approach could be less appropriate to implement health policy, but at least it is manageable and highly specific – screening procedures are standard ones. The approach developed in Pau da Lima, based on the use of micro-areas for screening social groups at risk according to their life chances, is indicated by the authors as useful in overcoming these difficulties. Through blueprint, standard procedures for screening micro-areas instead of individuals, the manageability and specificity of the risk approach can be approximated, hence providing an appropriate tool for the implementation of health policy. Then, the micro-areas represent an effective tool for 'marking out' groups of people at risk.

The actual homogeneity of the micro-areas is a crucial requisite in this respect. We said that the micro-areas are *relatively homogeneous*, because the differences internal to them are less significant than the differences between them. When a given micro-area is selected as a target, the possibility of making errors of inclusion and exclusion is limited, but not avoided at all. Some people who are actually at risk would be excluded from the target, and others who are not at risk would be included in it. We argue, however, that in a situation of scarcity of resources such as Pau da Lima individual screening procedures for the whole district's population are likely to determine even higher errors. The same procedures, instead, could be easily implemented in the prioritised micro-areas only, to mark out the subjects actually at risk within them.

Initial Conclusions on Primary Data Processing

The reliability of rapid appraisal data systematised into micro-areas was confirmed for most items. These data were not as precise as data generated by the household survey, but they could provide more holistic insights about local risks.

The overall validity of the micro-areas was also confirmed. The micro-areas actually reveal differences in local living conditions, which are relevant from an operational point of view. In this respect, the micro-areas are more precise and clear-cut categories than those previously used; they are also more manageable, as they can be easily interpreted and compared with each other, in order to take decisions in terms of priorities. The *bairros* were categories whose level of aggregation of data masked existing inequalities. The micro-area seems to represent the ideal level of disaggregation of data – an optimum balance between needs of detection of local inequalities and manageability.[4]

5.3 SECONDARY DATA PROCESSING

No specific problems existed for the systematisation and standardisation of secondary data, as these were already expressed in quantitative terms, and common and well-regulated procedures of data collection guaranteed their homogeneity.

However, these data could not be crossed in a simple and immediate way with data on living conditions. This cross-checking, in turn, was important to allow the health district management to interpret secondary data. These were collected in the district's health centres, and only referred to those residents who actually had access to the latter. Only by crossing these data with those on local living conditions – which covered the whole district's population – did it become possible to ascribe data on the use of health centres and epidemiological data to specific social groups.

Such a comparison between different data could be made through a common and specific territorial reference. Insofar as the territorial reference of data on living conditions was not specific and was internally heterogeneous – as was the case with the *bairro* – the comparison was impossible.

It became possible with the definition of the micro-areas. Data about local living conditions referred to social groups which were located in specific and clear-cut portions of the district's territory (the micro-areas). Data about patients registered in the health centres and epidemiological data referred to single individuals. However, these data could be related to each other through each patient's address. In this way, the data of each patient could be located in a given micro-area, and then associated to the socio-economic and environmental conditions of the latter. The geographic distribution of epidemiological data could be overlaid and compared to the geographic distribution of those local living conditions which could influence both the use of health services and the occurrence of ill-health events.

Secondary data could be referred also to the health centres' responsibility areas (HCRAs), as these were made up of different micro-areas. The HCRAs were defined according to the geographic barriers which influence the patients' flow and access to the health centres. An HCRA defines the area from which most of the patients of a health centre come – the health centre's constituency. Through the spatial reference of each patient, demand for health care to each health centre could be assessed, and properly managed by means of an appropriate health care supply.

Then, secondary data (epidemiological data and data on access to health care) were made meaningful and manageable by means of geographic references: to micro-areas, in order to associate them with data on living conditions; and to HCRAs, in order to manage the spontaneous demand for health care. Such geographic references were made possible when the original, and not specific territorial category – the *bairro* – was transformed as well as subdivided into more specific ones – the HCRAs and the micro-areas, respectively.

Due to the high number of records of secondary data, however, computerisation of information was an essential prerequisite for making these geographic references possible.

5.4 DATA COMPUTERISATION

Computerisation of data and maps was the last stage in knowledge-building in Pau da Lima. With computerisation, information which had been collected so far was structured into its final form and was made ready for use. By means of computerisation, different data were stored within a single information system, and enabled to dialogue with each other.

A Geographic Information System (GIS) was used to computerise the available data and maps. In a GIS all the available data – usually stored in a DBMS (data base management system) – are keyed to specific geographic locations.[5]

In Pau da Lima, secondary data (data on patients registered in the health centres and epidemiological data) were expressed as points on a map – single events which were located in the place of residence of each patient. Primary data, instead, were expressed as socio-economic and environmental thematic maps that referred to micro-areas and health centres' responsibility areas (HCRAs).

A GIS is usually provided with features such as the capacity to zoom in and out of specific portions of the map, to display different data values on a map by means of thematic maps, and to make queries about the available data, whereby only certain fields or values (for instance diarrhoeal diseases or infant deaths only) are displayed on the map. All these features were used in Pau da Lima to increase the capacity to analyse the available information.

Thematic maps for selected socio-economic and environmental indicators were prepared at both the HCRA and the micro-area level to allow comparison between the living conditions of different areas of the health district, and the association of these conditions with the health data. The most important aspects of living conditions – water, sanitation, income,[6] housing conditions – were displayed by means of thematic maps. These indicated with different colours the different degree of risk present of each area. They maps simplified data crossing and increased the analytical capacity of data users. Health data could be plotted, over the socio-economic and environmental thematic maps, permitting comparison of the spatial distribution of different variables.

System design and programming proceeded side by side and in close interaction with data processing. This was a productive interaction. On the one hand, system design and programming could be modelled on the real data which were being produced and processed, as well as on the actual needs of both data producers and data users. On the other hand, the technical requirements imposed by data computerisation stimulated a constant concern for the best way in which to format the available data. As well as a strict discipline, it fostered timeliness for data production and clarity of objectives for data processing.

A user-friendly application in Portuguese was developed by means of a compiler included in the original software package. This allowed the information system to be designed in a flexible way and according to the users' needs. This adaptation was due also to the interaction which occurred between system design and data collection and processing. Most important of all, flexibility was not obtained at the expense of discipline, precision, and specificity of the system. A menu was prepared with user-friendly commands to display and analyse the available information. In this way, a relatively limited number of options was made available to information users: a step-wise approach, or an 'analytic path' was created for data use and interpretation – a sort of 'one-best-way' for information use. In the next chapter we shall discuss to what extent this device was crucial for decision-making, as it simplified the analysis of the large amount of data available in the information system. It also allowed people with limited expertise in computers to have easy access to the information stored in the GIS.

Technical details and costs of the software and hardware which were used are reported in the Technical Appendix B.

5.5 DISCUSSION: FLEXIBILITY AND SPECIFICITY IN DATA PROCESSING

The problems of systematisation and standardisation of information which project management encountered at the end of data collection were basically solved for both primary and secondary data.

Primary data were systematised into territorial categories which were adequate to express relevant differences in local living conditions. The level of data disaggregation was satisfactory in terms of manageability. The common territorial reference of information was useful in making secondary data both meaningful and manageable. The manageability of information was further increased by means of data computerisation.

Information was treated so that its precision and manageability were substantially increased, thus approximating it to a specificity surrogate. A balanced blend of elements respectively from the blueprint and the process approach was necessary for that.

Process and flexibility

Elements of the process approach, responsible for flexibility in data processing, can be found in the gradual identification of the micro-areas, the definition of scores, and the information system design.

We consider the gradual construction of the categories (the micro-areas) in which the characteristics of the resident population were grouped. The provisional geographic grid used in the rapid appraisal, and the subsequent reports of the *bairros* were progressively refined by means of successive approximations (typical of a process approach), based on the recurrent reference of the available data to simple tables of comparison.

Moreover, the division of the district's territory into micro-areas was not based on existing administrative or geographic categories. On the contrary, it was from the analysis of the geographic distribution of local living conditions that the district's territory was subsequently subdivided into micro-areas. The result of this was a 'clever' map,[7] to be used to interpret the human geography of the territory rather than merely to reproduce its physical, geographic and administrative characteristics.

The micro-areas were the result of an attempt to *adapt* the information format to the local characteristics of Pau da Lima, as well as to the needs (for precision and manageability) of decision-makers. They were constructed from bottom-up indications and information about the real settlements which make up the urban and social network of Pau da Lima. Local knowledge of key informants was crucial in this respect, because it allowed a global, holistic view of the micro-areas under examination. This holistic view was important, as it provided insights into risks for the resident population as a whole.

The urban and social network of the health district was extremely complex and heterogeneous, and the whole process of knowledge-building in Pau da Lima can be seen as an interpretative effort aimed at ordering it, so as to make it manageable and precise through categorisation and systematisation.

Equally, standardisation by means of the attribution of scores was not guided by abstract and standard parameters, which would have been meaningless in the specific reality of the health district and useless for the project's purposes. Absolute scores, valid, for instance, for the city as a whole, would have been too aggregated for the local reality of the health district, and would have masked inequalities present in it. On the contrary, scores were defined by taking account exclusively of the limited and relative – but nonetheless crucial in terms of prioritisation – local reality of Pau da Lima. The capacity of key informants of ranking different social groups – to report differences in living conditions which *for them* were relevant, rather than precise absolute values – was also crucial. The process of attribution of scores was also adapted to this local perspective.

Data computerisation, too, presents elements of flexibility, as it occurred in close interaction with data processing.

Flexibility in the design and implementation of information systems is a critical condition for their successful use. According to Ingle, the initial needs assessment for the design of an information system must be conducted in a collaborative way; this carries much weight in the eventual acceptance of microcomputers by project staff.[8] The design team must acquire first-hand knowledge of the organisational needs and opportunities, and search for what is institutionally feasible rather than what is technically optimal.[9] These conditions, of flexibility and adaptation were basically satisfied in Pau da Lima.

The use of computers in information systems requires, and at the same time fosters, flexibility. Often computers are thought to be unsuitable for the treatment of rapid appraisal and qualitative data. It is argued that they give the 'false impression that "objective data" and "formal lines of communication" need to be emphasised to the exclusion or neglect of subjective and informal information'.[10] Yet, on the contrary, microcomputers seem to be particularly appropriate for qualitative fieldwork based on a flexible research design:

> qualitative research [...] emphasises diagnosis, not control, and interpretation, not explanation. [...] The microcomputer encourages closeness to the data and an intensive, interactive analytic style. This in turn may encourage a certain degree of methodological convergence as quantitative researchers find the detailed analysis of sub-populations easier and qualitative researchers are able to examine comparative contrasts within their material more fully.[11]

Blueprint and specificity

Elements of the blueprint approach were also present in data processing in Pau da Lima. The increased presence of these elements was responsible for the increased degree of precision and manageability of information. This was crucial in allowing information itself to become a specificity surrogate. We can find elements of the blueprint approach in both the process of data systematisation and standardisation and in data computerisation.

Tables of comparison and scores were used to transform the rapid appraisal data. These devices, although simplified, were of an analytic nature, as they implied a process of division of the mass of available data, and subsequent, recurrent interpretations of data presented in their new format.

Precise procedures were followed to systematise the available data, as each bit of information was analysed in depth from the rapid appraisal questionnaires and the reports, and cross-checked, by means of tables of comparison. Interpretation and comparison of data followed objective criteria and limited room was left to discretion as far as the territorial reference of information was concerned.

Systematic procedures were necessary also for the standardisation of data through the attribution of scores. Different situations of risk were methodically listed, compared, and then grouped. Specialised technical knowledge was necessary to assess different levels of risk and to rank them. Moreover, social interaction with the community was eliminated from both data systematisation and standardisation – the whole process was conducted by project staff alone.

Data computerisation imposed a strict discipline on data processing. Despite the flexibility in system design, the technical requirements imposed by data computerisation made the project staff aware of the need for a precise and clear-cut information format, and made the analytic treatment of data indispensable. Moreover, a user-friendly application with a limited number of options for information use was tailor-made according to the decision-makers' needs. But such an application, in its final form, was quite rigid and clear-cut, as it created an almost standardised path for the analysis of the data.

5.6 CONCLUSIONS

On the one hand, data processing maintained some characteristics of flexibility, due to the presence of elements from the process approach. Data processing was conducted in an adaptive way, and with creativity and experimentation.

On the other hand, more emphasis was given than previously to the use of elements from the blueprint approach. These elements were responsible for improvement in precision and manageability of information. This was treated systematically and analytically – it was necessary to codify, standardise and computerise it – and then it was turned into a more specific and manageable form. In this way, information became effectively usable for decision-making.

NOTES

1. F. Notarbartolo di Villarosa and A. Bunschaft, *A estruturação dos bairros da Região Urbana de Pau da Lima* (Salvador, Brazil: mimeo, 1990); F. Pedrão, *Urbanização, Informalidade e Saúde em Salvador* (Salvador, Brazil: mimeo, 1990).
2. E. de Kadt and R. Tasca, *Promovendo a Equidade: Um Novo Enfoque com Base no Setor Saúde* (São Paulo: Hucitec/Cooperação Italiana em Saúde, 1993), pp. 40–41.
3. Individual screening procedures can be quite inefficient in the use of the available resources. De Kadt and Tasca, quoting a study by Chen *et al.* on the measurement of child malnutrition and the subsequent risk of mortality, report that, for each malnourished child correctly detected as at risk, seven children are incorrectly detected. L.C. Chen *et al.*, *Classification of Energy-Protein Malnutrition by Anthropometry and Subsequent Risk of Mortality* (Bangladesh: International Centre for Diarrhoeal Disease, mimeo, 1978), p. 9, quoted by E. de Kadt and R. Tasca (1993), op. cit., p. 27.
4. De Kadt and Tasca identify three ways in which the population is usually categorised for the purpose of planning in public health:
   - by means of demographic variables (people who share certain individual characteristics such as the same age, gender, marital status etc., are a group);
   - by means of socio-economic variables (people who share certain characteristics derived from social processes, such as the same income, job, education etc., are a group);
   - by means of geographic/environmental areas (people who live within certain geographic/environmental boundaries are a group).

   According to the authors, the geographic approach has the advantage of using well-delimited, visible and physically reachable categories. However, areas defined in this way tend to be internally quite heterogeneous. Instead, people who share similar socio-economic conditions – people who are members of the same social class, or of another category with an equal sociological relevance – tend to show a relative homogeneity. The micro-areas have the main quality of the geographic approach – they represent clear-cut and comparable categories, defined on a territorial basis. But they are constructed through socio-economic indicators – they group people who share similar living conditions, hence showing a relative internal homogeneity. In a city with a spontaneous and uneven pattern of urbanisation such as Salvador, this relative homogeneity in living conditions in given spaces could be found *only in small areas* (E. de Kadt and R. Tasca (1993), op. cit., pp.36–40).
5. For further information on the use of GIS in development planning, see J. Dangermond, 'Geographic Information System Technology and Development Planning', *Regional Development Dialogue,* 11, 3 (1990), pp. 1–14, and B. Harris, 'Urban and Regional Planning in the Third World with a Geographic

Information System Support', *Regional Development Dialogue,* 11, 3 (1990), pp. 17–62; for specific applications in public health, see M.J.C. de Lepper, H.J. Scholten and R.M. Stern (eds.), *The Added Value of Geographical Information Systems in Public and Environmental Health* (Dordrecht, Boston, London: Kluwer Academic Publishers/WHO Regional Office for Europe, 1991).

6. We previously saw that data about income, although unreliable in terms of absolute values, are reliable in terms of ranking – they indicate who are respectively the 'richest' and the 'poorest' in Pau da Lima. The thematic maps visualised such a ranking instead of the absolute values.
7. The term 'clever map' to define the division of Pau da Lima into micro-areas was created by Eugênio Vilaça Mendes of PAHO.
8. M.D. Ingle, *Evaluating the Appropriateness of Microcomputers for Management Applications in Developing Countries* (New York: Development Project Management Centre, 1983), p. 20.
9. S.B. Peterson, 'Institutionalizing Microcomputers in Developing Bureaucracies: Theory and Practice from Kenya', *Information Technology for Development,* 5, 3 (1990b), p. 300.
10. M.D. Ingle (1983), op. cit., p. 32.
11. N.G. Fielding and R.G. Lee (eds), *Using Computers in Qualitative Research* (London: Sage, 1991), pp. 7–8.

6

Data Use for Decision-Making

6.1 INTRODUCTION TO DATA USE

In people-oriented activities, decisions about goals, targets, and means tend to be vague and ambiguous. These activities have an inherently low degree of specificity. This was the case in Pau da Lima at the beginning of the project.

In this chapter we assess to what extent decision-making improved as a result of the use of information which had been collected and processed during knowledge-building. We intend to see if information acted as an incentive to specificity (or as a specificity surrogate) in Pau da Lima. The hypothesis is that this occurred because the analytical use of information was made simple and information put effective pressures on decision-makers.

We analyse a decision-making process which took place in Pau da Lima during the HEAP (health, environment, and struggle against poverty) project. The project had among its goals the prioritisation of targets and the implementation of actions for the prevention of diarrhoeal diseases. Decisions in this respect were taken during an analytic exercise at the beginning of 1992. This exercise was specifically designed to test the impact of the information system use on decision-making. However, it was designed so as to be representative of strategic decision-making processes at the district managerial level in general.

The analysis is focused (a) on the quality of the decisions which were taken as the result of the use of the information system and (b) on some aspects of the interface between the information system itself and its users. The steps of the process of data use are analysed, and the procedures for targeting are examined, in order to assess the resulting degree of clarity and precision of targets, goals and means.

6.2 DECISION-MAKING BEFORE USE OF THE INFORMATION SYSTEM

Information was used and decisions had to be taken both before and in the course of the process of knowledge-building. It can be useful to analyse briefly some examples of decision-making at this stage of the project, in order to assess the quality of decisions taken before the information system was in use.

Decision-making at the Beginning of the Project

Information which had been collected by the health district management at the beginning of the project was used to produce a strategic plan.[1] This plan was meant to define the basic goals and guidelines for the development of the health district of Pau da Lima in the ensuing years, and to provide directives for daily management.

The first part of the plan was focused on the internal organisation of the health district. Goals and actions were set with regard to infrastructure, equipment, training, and the organisation of new services (such as epidemiological surveillance, reference systems, and so on). The plan was very detailed in this respect, and tasks, responsibilities, and deadlines were clearly indicated for each goal.

The second part of the plan was focused on the priority health problems of the health district. Five priority health problems were indicated:

- parasitic diseases in the age group 0–14 in the whole district;
- intestinal infections in the age group 0–14 in the whole district;
- nutritional problems in the age group 0–four, low-income families, in the whole district;
- skin diseases in the whole population resident near the city garbage dump (*bairro* of Cána Brava);
- respiratory diseases in the age group 0–four in Cana Brava.

These problems were analysed according to different criteria (impact, epidemiological potential, technology required to tackle them and costs). Their determinants were analysed also – from general determinants at the societal level to specific causes both internal to the health district organisation (such as lack of personnel) and external to it (such as lack of sanitation). Finally, possible solutions for each problem and its determinants were indicated, at both the sectoral and inter-sectoral level. However, neither tasks nor responsibilities were defined to implement actions.

A valuable effort was made by the health district management to formulate this plan – especially because poor data were available. Both the health problems and the solutions which were identified were probably correct. But the plan left the reader with the feeling of something obvious and abstract. It lacked a thorough analysis of the way in which certain problems occurred in the specific context of Pau da Lima – consequently, it was impossible to assess the actual feasibility of possible solutions, and to design specific actions. Most important of all, *no real priorities were set*: it was clear, in fact, that all the problems which had been prioritised could not be tackled simultaneously in the whole district. The targets were still too vague for feasible actions: the age group 0–14 for the health district as a whole was still too general a target – it represented 37.3 per cent of the district population – as well as the age group 0–four of low-income families (families which represented more than 60 per cent of the health district population). Most important of all, no operational indications were provided for 'marking out' the subjects effectively at risk. A specific target group was defined only when a social group was clearly related to a geographic area (Cana Brava, 4,700 inhabitants).

In general, the plan was quite precise and concrete in its first part, which referred to the internal organisation of the health district. This was the 'blueprint' part of the plan. But in its second part, the 'outward-oriented' or 'demand-oriented' part, which referred to people, needs and targets, it showed a certain vagueness.

Decision-making in the Course of Knowledge-building

The whole process of knowledge-building in Pau da Lima was meant to overcome the deficiencies of the information which had been generated and used to support the original health district plan. New data began to be available from the end of 1989 on, and could be used on some opportunities.

An example of this use was an immunisation campaign which took place in March 1990. The impact of the new data on the campaign's organisation was contradictory. On the one hand, the regional directorate of the state health secretariat, which was in charge of the overall management of the campaign, refused to use the new demographic data which had been provided by the health district management of Pau da Lima – instead, it kept on using old and wrong data. On the other hand, more resources were given to the health district management (mobile immunisation units, cars with loud-speakers and pamphlets for advertising the campaign). These resources were concentrated in the micro-areas which had already been defined as 'at risk' and with little access to the health centres. No formal evaluation was made, but participants in the campaign reported that more people than previously received vaccines in areas where coverage had always been low.

More general indications came from several meetings between the health district and the project management. In these meetings the output in terms of decisions was often low and vague. Targets and actions were often defined according to standard norms for typical 'vertical' programmes (for instance immunisation, maternal and child health care), with little effort to define these actions according to the specific context of Pau da Lima. General target groups were identified, with no indications on how to mark them out and where to concentrate the available resources. Moreover, difficulties emerged with regard to the systematic, analytic use of information: those data which were gradually made available were not systematically crossed with each other to try to identify more specific target groups.

From the case of the immunisation campaign and from these meetings, the need to use the new data more systematically emerged, as well as to make the data themselves more 'convincing' and capable of putting 'pressures' on decision-makers. For that, it was argued, the information system which was being implemented would be helpful. Because of the lack of analytic capacity which had emerged, moreover, it was decided to prepare a pre-established 'analytic path' with limited options in the information system's menu. When the system was ready for use, then, it was decided to start a systematic exercise for its use in decision-making. The opportunity came when a plan had to be prepared for the new HEAP project.

6.3 DATA USE AND DECISION-MAKING

The HEAP project was an experimental project, conducted in three different Brazilian states (Bahia, Ceará and Minas Gerais). It was aimed at experimenting with and implementing actions which tackled priority health problems by acting on their determinants related to poverty and the environment. The information system of Pau da Lima was particularly interesting for the project, because it was focused on the relations between health problems and their environmental and socio-economic determinants.

Data Analysis

A systematic exercise for the use of the information system was programmed to support the preparation of the HEAP project plan in Pau da Lima.[2] The problem of diarrhoeal diseases was chosen as the priority health problem to tackle. It was selected both because of its high incidence in Pau da Lima, and because a cholera epidemic was spreading in North-eastern Brazil, and was about to reach Salvador. As no cases of cholera had yet been detected, it was decided to use diarrhoeal diseases as a proxy for it. This was also an appropriate problem for the exercise, because of its strong association with poverty and bad environmental conditions.

The exercise was structured into regular meetings, in which different analytic steps were followed, according to a logical sequence of use of the information system. Project staff participated in the exercise until targets were defined – from that moment on, the health district management continued alone for the design and implementation of specific actions.

The participants in the exercise of information use for decision-making were the sociologist, the epidemiologist and the computer engineer from the project staff, and the health district manager together with two epidemiologists from the health district staff.

The following indicators were used for targeting:

- Socio-economic and environmental indicators: diarrhoeal diseases are transmitted by water, which, in turn, is contaminated because of the lack of sanitation. Therefore, targets had to be defined according to the situation of water and sanitation. The variable income was used too, as a general and multipurpose indicator of socio-economic conditions.[3]

- Health indicators: data on diarrhoeal diseases and access to the health centres.

- Demographic indicators: target groups had to be small in order to be specific and to allow the definition and implementation of simple and manageable activities.

Through a combination of these indicators, it was argued that decision-makers would be able to 'mark out' specific and geographically well-delimited target groups.

The selected indicators were analysed, then, by means of the Geographic Information System (GIS). Their spatial distribution was displayed by means of thematic maps.[4]

The analysis was conducted initially at the level of the health centres' responsibility areas (HCRAs). Four HCRAs emerged as the most disadvantaged according to socio-economic and environmental criteria. These were the HCRAs of Dom Avelar, Cana Brava, Jardim Nova

Esperança and Nova Brasília. The total population of these HCRAs was 35,210 (23.7 per cent of the district's population). This result was partially confirmed when the data on diarrhoeal diseases were overlaid to the socio-economic and environmental thematic maps.

When the rate of incidence of these diseases was considered instead of their geographic distribution on a map, only the HCRAs of Nova Brasília and Cana Brava appeared as at risk. Nevertheless, the distribution on the map of data on the access to the health care services indicated that in most HCRAs only a small percentage of the resident population was registered in the health centres. This meant that in most cases the available health data reflected the health conditions of just a small part of the population. Then, strong biases in health data, due to a non-homogeneous access to health care services, were quite likely. Moreover, it was interesting to notice that the HCRAs which, according to the previous analysis, were the most at risk (Cana Brava and Nova Brasília), were also those with the lowest rate of access. The hypothesis was formulated, then, that the socio-economic dynamics which determined a given pattern of risk and disease could be influential for the pattern of access, too – but how and why? Was the (low) access to the health services homogeneously distributed among the different social groups which resided in the different micro-areas of the HCRAs, or was this not so? Moreover, who were those who actually did not use the local health services, the poorest or the better-off? In very poor areas, the possible lack of access by the (few) better-off could not determine such a low aggregated access rate. Therefore, we could argue that, in these areas, the large majority of the poor had little or no access to health care. However, this was of little operational use, unless we could localise the micro-areas in which such access was the lowest.

In order to try to answer this question, environmental and socio-economic data, health data, and data on access had to be crossed with each other at a micro level – that is, at a level which reflected more precisely the local living conditions. The analysis had to focus, then, on the micro-area level, and had to work with geographically referenced data, instead of tables and rates (these, in fact, would have no statistical representativeness at the micro-area level, due to the small number of cases and the reduced dimension of the universe).

When the geographic distribution of data was analysed at the level of the micro-areas, a more heterogeneous socio-economic and environmental picture emerged than in the analysis at the HCRA level. Most important, some extreme situations were displayed, which previously had been masked by aggregated data.

The micro-areas were ranked, then, according to the values of their socio-economic and environmental indicators. The resulting rank was divided into quartiles, and only the first two quartiles were selected as possible targets. The micro-areas in the first quartile represented micro-areas 'at high risk', those in the second quartile micro-areas at 'moderate risk'. The population of the former was 8,637 (5.82 per cent of the district's population), that of the latter 33,176 (22.33 per cent of the district's population) – a slightly higher percentage than that resulting from the analysis at the HCRA level, but much more focused on the most disadvantaged situations in the health district.

Even after this initial selection, in fact, we could see that *all* the HCRAs had micro-areas at risk. This reinforced the argument that aggregated data at the HCRA level tended to mask existing situations of vulnerability, especially in large HCRAs. Whilst the single scores of the most disadvantaged micro-areas could influence the aggregated score of small HCRAs, such an influence could not be perceived in large HCRAs. In the previous analysis, in fact, the small HCRAs (Cana Brava, Nova Brasília, Dom Avelar and Jardim Nova Esperança) could be classified as at risk – but this was not possible with the large HCRAs, in which specific and micro situations of risk were lost.

After the micro-areas were ranked according to socio-economic and environmental criteria, the exercise proceeded to the analysis of health data. Each HCRA was zoomed in with the GIS, and both data on diarrhoeal diseases and data on the access to the health centres were plotted on the maps. In this way, the spatial distribution of these data could be compared, for each selected micro-area, with the spatial distribution of socio-economic and environmental data.

Targeting

As a result of the previous analysis, health data could immediately confirm the presence of socio-economic and environmental risks in five micro-areas. All these micro-areas could be confirmed as at risk, because of the simultaneous presence, in them, of poor socio-economic and environmental conditions, of a high concentration of diseases, and of a homogeneous spatial distribution, in their HCRAs, of access to the health centres (which indicated that the data on diseases were not biased). Consequently, these micro-areas could be selected as 'certain' targets. The total population of these micro-areas was 18,010 (12.12 per cent of the health district's population).

In contrast, data on diseases could neither confirm nor reject the presence of socio-economically and environmentally conditioned risks, in the other micro-areas detected as possible targets. Doubts persisted with regard to these micro-areas, because in most of them health data were hardly available, due to the scarce or absent access of their residents to the health care services. It was impossible to assess, then, if the low occurrence of reported cases of disease was due to the lack of actual cases, or to biases in health data collection. In this case, we assumed that – unless the contrary could be proved – socio-economic and environmental data were more important than health data, because of the scarce reliability and validity of the latter. More precisely, for most of these micro-areas we assumed that the same socio-economic and environmental factors that could determine a high risk of contracting diseases prevented also the wide access of residents to health care services, and thus the probability of their being detected as at risk by the latter, hence inducing a bias in the health data referring to them.

In other words, we aimed at providing our empirical conclusions with some degree of certainty, by 'triangulating' on the maps socio-economic and environmental data and data on diseases, and by assessing the reliability of the latter through cross-checks with data on access. Only when all these indicators seemed to coincide, were the micro-areas selected for targeting. This search for certainty and confirmation, in turn, was aimed at reducing the probability of making errors of exclusion (of micro-areas at risk) and inclusion (of micro-areas not at risk) in targeting.

In the first set of micro-areas – where all kinds of data coincided – the possibility of making errors of inclusion was reduced: micro-areas showing bad socio-economic and environmental indicators, together with bad but reliable disease indicators, were likely to be actually at risk.

In the second set of micro-areas – where socio-economic and environmental indicators did not coincide with health indicators, but the latter were not reliable due to possible biases from the lack of access to health care services – further interpretations were necessary. When the analysis indicated the probability of biases in this respect, the micro-areas were selected for targeting, in order to limit the possibility of errors of exclusion.

At the end of the exercise, 11 micro-areas were selected as target areas for the prevention of diarrhoeal diseases. These micro-areas came from the following HCRAs: Nova Brasília (two micro-areas), Cana Brava (two), Jardim Nova Esperança (two), Sete de Abril (two), Pau da Lima (one), Dom Avelar (one), and UMO Castelo Branco (one).

Assessment of Precision in Targeting

We can see that seven out of eleven of the micro-areas selected for targeting came from the four HCRAs previously indicated as at risk (Nova Brasília, Cana Brava, Jardim Nova Esperança and Dom Avelar), whilst the other four micro-areas came from the other HCRAs. This did not mean that the conclusions of the analysis at the HCRA level were *wrong* – rather, this meant that the present ones were *more precise*. In this case it was specifically indicated what parts of the HCRAs at risk were 'more at risk'; and other micro-areas were also indicated, which had been masked and then lost by the previous, aggregated data of larger HCRAs.

The micro-areas selected for targeting had a population of 23,475 – which represented 15.8 per cent of the district's population. This was a smaller target group than the one previously identified in the HCRAs' analysis, which represented 24 per cent of the district's population.

These micro-areas represented a very precise target group – that is, a small group in which risks were highly concentrated. In fact, from the available data we calculated that 72 per cent of the district's inhabitants with the worst situation with regard to drinkable water, as well as 55 per cent of those with the worst sanitation, resided in the selected micro-areas. The micro-areas were more specific, with regard to environmental risks, than the HCRAs. The same figures for the selected HCRAs, in fact, were 32 per cent for both water and sanitation.[5]

Implications for High-specificity of a Precise Targeting

Through the analysis conducted at the micro-area level, very precise, well-delimited, and physically reachable target groups were identified and 'marked out'. The conditions were provided to increase at least the allocative efficiency of the actions for the prevention of diarrhoeal diseases, as these could be concentrated in those micro-areas where the risks were greater, and where the possibility of maximising their impact was higher.

Through a micro-localised targeting, the '*potential for specification*' was increased of people-oriented activities to prevent diarrhoeal diseases in Pau da Lima.[6]

The analytical focus at the micro level, together with the capacity of the GIS of zooming in the maps and overlaying different indicators, were crucial factors. By analysing more in depth the selected micro-areas, targeting could be made even more precise, clearer goals could be identified, and actions could be tailor-made according to the peculiar context of each micro-area.

According to Israel, one of the ways to simulate high specificity is to simplify objectives and to reduce the range of alternative methods.[7] In the present case, this goal was achieved by means of a micro-localised approach. In the first step, clear-cut and visible targets (the selected micro-areas) were identified. In the second step, these were zoomed in and analysed in depth; targets and goals were specified further, and the local risks and resources could be considered closely, so that a clearer framework was set to discuss the possible alternatives of action.

Two examples in the areas which turned out to be at higher risk might be interesting in this respect.

Community Health Workers in Nova Brasília

A first example comes from a programme of community health workers (CHWs) in Nova Brasília. The CHWs made regular home visits, educating mothers in preventive as well as simple curative measures, and collecting data on the occurrence of communicable diseases. The CHWs' activities were concentrated in those micro-areas which were defined as at risk. Each CHW was the responsible for a few streets within a given micro-area – home visits were made more frequently in those streets which showed the highest occurrence of diseases. In addition, indications could be provided for the individual monitoring of children at risk of diarrhoeal diseases, by displaying on the maps only those cases of diarrhoea among children younger than one year. When points of concentration appeared, they could be enlarged, so that the particular homes where diseases had occurred would show up more clearly, and more frequent visits could be oriented towards them. In this way, the CHWs could be provided with clear targets and goals, as well as precise guidelines to orient their actions. Moreover, their work could be more easily monitored and supervised.

This capacity of pre-orienting the CHWs' activities and of concentrating them on specific, well-delimited and physically reachable targets could be useful in supporting training and visit health programmes. The training and visit method is based on principles similar to the ones adopted in Pau da Lima. It lets clients express their needs through a close interaction with the project; it defines a small number of impact points on which to concentrate the interventions; and it aims at clarifying the objectives of the interventions through simplification.[8] When used for family planning, health and nutrition (PHN), the training and visit system prioritises by using a blend of epidemiological and subjective needs, and it orients the interventions towards a few, selected clients, where a maximum impact can be obtained.[9]

However, the training and visit system imposes a heavy managerial burden on the local health services, because of the need for a strict supervision of field activities. The possibility of focusing these activities on very precise and small targets, according to the method described here, could partly reduce such a burden. One of the basic principles of the training and visit system – the principle of selecting a few clients at risk to be followed up by the outreach workers – could be strengthened, and its implementation could be made easier, by a tool such as the information system developed in Pau da Lima. The preliminary problem of detecting and marking out the subjects at risk does not seem to be solved by the application of the training and visit system for PHN. As we previously discussed, the individual screening procedures which are usually adopted are prone to frequent errors. They are also resource-intensive, due to the need for an at least initial 'blanket' coverage of the territory. By identifying, instead, the micro-areas at risk, and then progressively zooming them in, this preliminary problem could be partially solved. Subsequently, the activities of the outreach workers could be further concentrated on those streets and even households, where the risks are actually more apparent. Fewer field-workers, and then fewer supervisors, would be required for covering a given area, because their performance would be made more efficient by selecting just very small and specific portions of the area as a whole in which to work.

Inter-Sectoral Actions in Cana Brava

Another interesting example comes from Cana Brava. Cana Brava was selected as the site for a set of inter-sectoral activities to be co-ordinated by the HEAP project. Four types of actions were programmed: sanitation, habitation improvements, drainage, and garbage removal. An inter-sectoral group was created to plan and manage the execution of the activities. This group was made up of four representatives from the community, and four officials from different institutions – namely, the municipal secretariat of health, the state company of water and sanitation (EMBASA), the municipal company for garbage removal (LIMPURB), and the municipal secretariat of infrastructure. This group managed the execution of the following activities: garbage removal with community labour, improvements in public garbage collection, recuperation of the water system and periodic control of the quality of water, garbage recycling and production of recycled paper (these latter activities were meant also to generate income for the community).

Inter-sectoral actions were actually implemented in Cana Brava. Inter-sectorality was operationalised from the bottom-up rather than through formal agreements at the municipal level, as well as inductively, through the collective identification of concrete problems, commonly felt at the local level, around which resources could be mobilised and integrated actions co-ordinated. Sharing different information on a geographic overlay of common responsibility was crucial for that.[10]

Cana Brava was not only one of the most vulnerable areas of Pau da Lima – it was also the most visible and politically critical, because of the presence of the garbage dump of Salvador. The case of Cana Brava was shown by the health district management to the municipal level. Data from the information system on the association between poor environmental conditions and bad health indicators were exhibited, increasing further the visibility of local problems. As a result, Cana Brava was chosen by the municipal secretariat of planning to receive funds from the federal government, equivalent to US$ 3.5 millions, for a wide-ranging project of sanitation. As stated during a regional meeting to evaluate the HEAP project, each dollar invested by the latter in Pau da Lima generated about $30 of funds received from other sources. The increased visibility of problems together with the indication of clear targets and goals, obtained through the use of the information system, were formally recognised as influential factors in this respect.[11]

Some comments are pertinent here with regard to these two examples. First, more resources were actually invested in the areas which were at higher risk. Second, when we put the actions which were programmed in these areas on an hypothetical 'curative/preventive' or 'sectoral/inter-sectoral' continuum, these tend to stay, respectively, on the 'preventive' and 'inter-sectoral' (that is, on the more 'people-oriented') side.

In these examples specific goals could be defined and tailor-made actions designed, thanks to the micro focus which had been used to analyse the micro-areas. Activities could be kept simple, because their goals were equally simple and small. General and complex goals for the district as a whole could be simplified and turned into concrete targets and goals at the micro-area level, and actions could be designed accordingly and appropriately for each local context.[12]

Equally, the community and institutions from sectors other than health could be motivated to participate in programmes at the grassroots level, when precise, clear, and really local problems were turned into targets and goals. Local residents, especially, tended to feel these problems as 'really theirs', as they had participated in their definition during the rapid appraisal.

Performance of the Health Services

We can try to assess if the use of the information system had any direct effect on the performance of the health care services in Pau da Lima.

Between 1988 and 1993 there was an overall but erratic increase in productivity of medical services in the health centres of the district. This is shown in Table 6.1.

This growth in productivity was due to such factors as improvement of the health centres, provision of equipment, allocation of new personnel, training, and implementation of routines for medical treatment. None of these factors can be related directly to the use of the information system. However, the health centres' supply of services was defined by the health district management according to the epidemiological characteristics of the population of each health centre's constituency. These characteristics, in turn, could be known and became effectively supportive of decision-making only when the HCRAs were defined and appropriately analysed.

TABLE 6.1
PRODUCTIVITY IN MEDICAL SERVICES[13] IN THE HEALTH DISTRICT OF PAU DA LIMA, 1988–93

YEAR	PRODUCTIVITY
1988	22.5 per cent
1989	19.4 per cent
1990	53.9 per cent
1991	43.8 per cent
1992	59.2 per cent
1993	53.1 per cent

(*Source:* Health District of Pau da Lima)

The HCRAs were defined in 1989 (during the rapid appraisal), and the health centres were reorganised accordingly in the same year and in 1990. As a matter of fact, a quantum jump in productivity occurred between 1989 and 1990 – no other factors can explain this beyond the reorganisation based on the division of the district into HCRAs.

After 1990, productivity remained almost stable, and – in absolute terms – quite low. This was due to such factors as low salaries and problems with the maintenance of equipment, as well as with the supply of drugs and other materials. These were factors which could not be solved by the district level alone. Their solution, instead, was dependent upon wider managerial reforms which should take place at the municipal and state level. However, deficiencies can be detected at the district level too. The managerial capacity at the health centre level continued to be quite weak. The decision-making capacity of the personnel of the health centres showed no improvement, as they did not become fully involved in the discussion with the health district management on organisational issues. The participation of the directors of the health centres in the executive commission of the health district was clearly insufficient in this respect.

Most important of all, the use of the information system remained limited to the health district management and to the personnel employed by the project. This was due to the lack of human resources for using the computer in the health centres, as well as to the lack of time and motivation by the doctors.[14] Consequently, the professionals of the health centres were not informed about the actual needs of their constituencies (HCRAs). Moreover, the lack of use of the GIS at the health centre level was crucial, as the professionals working in the former did not receive any indication or 'pressure' to orient and improve their daily activities.

The supply of health services improved initially, thanks to a general rearrangement by the health district management. This rearrangement was oriented by the definition of the HCRAs and by the knowledge of their characteristics and needs. However, the productivity of the health services did not improve further, both because of general factors outside the health district management control, and because of an insufficient decentralisation in the use of the information system. This provided the professionals in the health centres with no tools to support their daily decision-making process, and with no feedback about the effect of their activities. Due to incorrect organisational arrangements, an important resource of the information system as a specificity surrogate was not diffused in the health centres of the district.

Impact on the Health Conditions of the Population

It is always difficult to assess the impact of a given set of actions on the health conditions of a target group, as it is usually hard to isolate the effect of the variables under study from the effect of other, external factors. However, some indications in this respect can be obtained from the evidence of our case-study.

In Table 6.2 we consider the evolution of diarrhoeal diseases in 1991, 1992 and 1993 (first semester). The exercise to test the use of the information system took place at the beginning of 1992, and used data from 1991.

Only in two HCRAs (Nova Brasília and Cana Brava) was there a constant reduction in the incidence of diarrhoeal diseases over the period. In the other HCRAs, either the trend is uncertain, stable or upwards.

Nova Brasília and Cana Brava were the HCRAs which had been previously identified as the most at risk, and preventive and promotional activities (CHWs and inter-sectoral interventions) were concentrated in four of their micro-areas. These actions took place *outside* the health centres, and involved professionals who effectively used the information system, or at least were familiar with the approach based on the micro-localisation of problems and actions. The reduction of diarrhoeal diseases in these areas seems to indicate that the use of the system and the familiarity with the approach contributed to a correct allocation of resources, and to a successful implementation of people-oriented activities in the field.

Even so, the aggregate rate of incidence for the health district as a whole did not improve substantially between 1991 and 1993. This probably indicates the need (a) to continue with the actions already undertaken (the incidence rate of Cana Brava was still too high); and (b) to mobilise further resources, and to replicate these actions in the other micro-areas of the district which had been selected as a target.

TABLE 6.2
INCIDENCE OF DIARRHOEAL DISEASES (PERCENTAGE EACH 100,000 INHABITANTS) IN THE HCRAs OF PAU DA LIMA, 1991, 1992, 1993 (FIRST SEMESTER)

HCRA	1991	1992	1993
Pau da Lima	90.8	383.7	189.0
Castelo Branco	191.4	538.8	27.3
Dom Avelar	285.5	203.9	279.0
Nova Brasília	1327.5	998.7	181.8
Cana Brava	1646.6	527.8	464.4
Sete de Abril	246.4	584.3	246.4
Jd. Nova Esperança	209.8	151.5	314.7
Health district	**262.4**	**446.8**	**227.4**

(*Source:* Health District of Pau da Lima)

Moreover, specific interventions for the treatment of diarrhoeal diseases, such as training in oral rehydration therapy, were undertaken in *all* the health centres of the district. Apparently, even these interventions did not have an effect on the aggregate figure for the district as a whole. This seems to be consistent with the low increase in productivity and with the related, limited use of the information system which we previously analysed.

In conclusion, we suggest that the use of the information system produced positive effects when it was diffused among the professionals involved in the activities which the system itself was meant to support. This was the case with some typically people-oriented activities implemented outside the health centres. In contrast, only the reorganisation of the health centres according to the characteristics of their HCRAs had some effect on the productivity of the health services. We cannot assess the possible impact of the use of the information system in this respect, as this was not diffused among the professionals working in the health centres.

The Use of the Information System

The exercise of data analysis for decision-making was the final step of a process during which the information system was gradually accepted, and finally used, by the health district management.

In the previous chapters we saw that the project's personnel had been employed extensively for knowledge-building. In contrast, the health district management had to be fully involved and trained in data use, as it was its staff which had to learn to utilise the information system, in order to improve its decision-making capacity.[15]

Initially the health district management was neither completely convinced about nor fully involved in the issue of the information system. Although it had participated in the information system design, its involvement in the whole process of knowledge-building had been too marginal to produce real consensus and commitment. Possibly this had been a mistake on the part of the project management – although it can be partly justified if we consider the short time available to them for producing concrete results, and, conversely, the long time required for the health district to mobilise its own resources for knowledge-building. In such a situation of lack of consensus and commitment, the requests by the project management to start an exercise on the use of the information system were initially perceived by the health district management as an unwelcome extra burden. However, these attitudes gradually changed, certain elements being influential in this respect.

Notwithstanding the lack of commitment on the part of some members of the health district management, the communication flow between them and the project management was never interrupted. The continuity of personnel on both sides was crucial in this respect.

Moreover, PAHO's HEAP project provided the health district management with autonomous funds to be spent on preventing the occurrence of diarrhoeal diseases in Pau da Lima. For the first time the health district management had to take concrete decisions with regard to planning and targeting. The need for instruments to support decision-making, which had been quite abstract so far, was turned into a real demand.

The project management gradually succeeded in gaining legitimacy vis-à-vis the health district management. By 1991 the project management had started to collaborate with PAHO on the issue of information systems. This collaboration eventually led to the project management being asked to help other Brazilian municipalities to set up similar systems. This gave the project management a degree of prestige, which helped its acceptance as a legitimate partner by the whole health district management.

As a result of this, all the members of the health district management became convinced that it would be useful to participate actively in the exercise of data use proposed by the project management. But only when these conditions (that is, the earned legitimacy of the project management, and the emergence of a real need for data use by the health district management) were satisfied, did traditional managerial tools such as training and supervision become effective instruments for increasing the degree of commitment and motivation of the health district management with regard to the information system use.

Conclusions on Data Analysis

As a result of the information system use, the quality of decisions improved in Pau da Lima.

The user-friendliness of the information system did not require any sophisticated skills in computing. The analytic use of data was eased, as different variables could be crossed with each other, through a common reference to the same geographic overlay. Simple tables and data bases were also used. This produced common-sense decisions, supported by appropriate data, which proved adequate for health district management.

Information acted as an effective incentive to specificity – or as a specificity surrogate – in decision-making. This conclusion refers to a single exercise with a few participants. This obviously limits the degree of generalisation of our results. In order to produce impact on the health district's organisational behaviour and performance as a whole, information should be used recurrently over time, as well as by more participants (especially the professionals in the health centres). We have no guarantees that the use of information will actually be institutionalised without the constant support of the expatriate staff – although we have no specific reasons to suspect that this will not occur either.[16] Such support, in fact, was crucial in implementing the information system and in training the health district management in its use. However, once the latter had been trained, and once the benefits deriving from the use of the information system had become visible, no further external support was required.

These limitations notwithstanding, the results of the analytical exercise provided promising indications on the ability of information to become an effective specificity surrogate in Pau da Lima.

6.4 DISCUSSION: FLEXIBILITY AND SPECIFICITY IN DECISION-MAKING

The quality of decisions improved in Pau da Lima as a consequence of better use of the available information. Precise targets and goals were defined, and people-oriented actions were implemented successfully. The overall result was an increase in the 'potential for specificity' of some of the activities of the health district.

We argue that this was due to the strong presence of elements of the blueprint model, regulating the decision-making process. The role of the process approach and of its main quality – flexibility – was substantially reduced. Standard procedures were set for data use and analysis. The options which were given to data users were quite limited. Data interpretation was still necessary, of course, but it was framed by a few, clear, and simple alternatives.

At the beginning of decision-making the tools to be used had been set already, as well as the way in which they had to be used. This 'one-best-way' of doing things is typical of the blueprint approach. In this way, decision-makers were provided with clear and easily comprehensible alternatives for targeting and programming activities, as well as with the capacity of assessing the variable degree of certainty or validity of each possible alternative. In sum: they were provided with clear indications to follow.

The foundations for that had already been laid in data processing, when the territory had been divided into micro-areas. But the use of the geographic information system produced further peculiar and decisive effects in terms of specificity. These effects regarded mainly the aspects of data use, which we analyse in-depth in the following sections.

Simplification, Codification and Agreement

In Chapter 2 we discussed the widespread reluctance of decision-makers to use information. These problems were also met in Pau da Lima. Despite the availability of manageable information, the project staff had to undertake an analytical exercise explicitly aimed at fostering the use of the information system. The results of this exercise were satisfactory, and information actually had an impact on decision-making. What were the factors, then, that produced this impact, and that put pressure on decision-makers?

One such factor was simplification. Several authors stress the importance of simplicity in decision-making processes.

Moris argues that it is necessary to simplify scientific solutions to problems into decision rules that can be applied routinely without special expertise. According to him 'learning is more likely to occur by framing alternative hypotheses than by seeking ever greater degrees of certainty in regard to a single hypothesis'.[17] A plea for a simplification of intellectual tasks is also made by Lindblom.[18] Moreover, planners' time has a high opportunity cost, and would be misused if applied to sophisticated modelling.[19]

In the course of knowledge-building, a conscious effort was undertaken to simplify and organise the heterogeneous and complex reality of Pau da Lima, in order to make information about its living conditions more comprehensible and manageable. During decision-making, in turn, an equally conscious effort was undertaken to simplify and codify the procedures for the use of this information.

Simplicity characterised decision-making in Pau da Lima. The operations conducted were easy, and did not require sophisticated skills. The use of a computer allowed the provision of precise, standard and codified guidelines for data use and analysis, by means of an interface with limited, pre-established options. Simplification, in other words, contributed to setting and codifying a 'one-best-way' of analysing data. This, in turn, facilitated and at the same time stimulated data use, and created the conditions that allowed information to have impact on decision-making.

Unambiguous and manageable information, together with standard and codified procedures for its use, provided decision-makers in Pau da Lima with precise indications about targets and goals; we have some evidence that clear alternatives of action were provided as well, with regard to the means for attaining these goals. In this way, agreement at least on targets and goals was promoted in Pau da Lima. This, in turn, fostered specificity and discipline. These, in fact, are obtained by the agreement that standard and codified procedures foster with regard to the way of 'doing things'.

Israel uses the Thompson–Tuden matrix to classify different types of decisions. According to this matrix, decisions are classified on two axes, agreement–disagreement about objectives and agreement–disagreement about methods. In low-specificity activities there is disagreement about both objectives and methods – therefore, decisions are of the 'inspirational type'. When agreement is reached at least about the objectives, 'judgement' decisions are taken. When there is agreement about both objectives and methods, finally, decisions of the 'computation' type are taken.[20]

In Pau da Lima, agreement was reached about objectives and targets. We have tried to make a case for the argument that, as a consequence of this and of designing simple actions by 'zooming in' at the micro-area level, agreement about methods could also be reached – although we have no systematic evidence of that. Therefore, decisions in Pau da Lima reached at least the 'judgement' status.

Motivation

Knowledge-building in Pau da Lima tried to build up adequate channels for the expression of needs, and to open up the health district to the demands from the external environment.

However, once these external signals are perceived by an organisation, they must be acknowledged by decision-makers, and put pressure on them. In this respect, as Leibenstein puts it, the translation of external into internal signals must be efficient, effective, and consistent with the organisational aims.[21] The simplification and codification of the procedures for information system use are aimed at facilitating such a translation.

According to Leibenstein, information has both an informational and a motivational content. The latter determines 'constraint concern' to the participants. Motivational inputs of information cannot be neglected, because – as this author argues – learning from experience is more likely when pressures are high.

In Pau da Lima the information system use was successful in increasing the decisions' clarity and precision, because it imposed pressures or constraint concern on the participants. These pressures were facilitated by the factors we previously saw – simplification, standardisation, and agreement. But a further factor was crucial – visibility. When the established procedures for data analysis were followed, the visibility and the relevance of local problems was increased, by displaying in a comprehensible way apparent inequalities and likely associations between the patterns of diseases and of risks. In this way, data became more convincing, and had impact on decision-making.

The Role of Technology

The micro-localised approach developed in Pau da Lima was crucial for increasing the visibility of local problems. But we formulate the hypothesis that the use of GIS technology was also critical.

In Chapter 1 we saw that, according to both Hirschman[22] and Israel,[23] successful projects are high-tech ones, as technology imposes discipline or specificity on participants – as we said, a one-best-way of doing things. In Pau da Lima, a sophisticated technology such as GIS was employed to support decision-making. Notwithstanding its sophistication, this technology made possible the development of a user-friendly, tailor-made application, including an interface with limited, pre-established options. This allowed the codification of the procedures for data use and analysis, and rendered the latter easier. Moreover, the GIS made data more visual and intuitive, and increased the visibility of local problems through the display of their spatial distribution.

However, a further aspect was crucial with regard to the use of technology in decision-making. In Chapter 1 we discussed the argument that the technology core of organisations tends to perform well in LDCs, as it can be buffered from the external environment. The lack of external interference allows processes within this technical core to work according to standard, blueprint procedures. This is what occurred in Pau da Lima, where the decision-making process, because of its technological support, was to some extent buffered from the external environment and from social interaction with both the community and the political levels, and so could follow technical criteria, hence producing high-quality decisions.

However, this neither implies that the properly political aspects were excluded *tout court* from decision-making in Pau da Lima, nor that the decisions taken at the technical level were automatically accepted, and then implemented, by the political level or the community. Fortunately, no information system could produce such results. We argue, in contrast, that decisions with good technical foundations could be taken by managers, and then recommended to and negotiated with, both the political level and the community. These decisions, in turn, were supported by clear and convincing data, which provided an appropriate framework for setting in a clear-cut way the terms of the negotiation.

Extra-technical Aspects of Data Use

Notwithstanding the importance of the just mentioned technical aspects, other elements, of a non-technical nature, were crucial for the information system use and for producing impact on decision-making.

Several political, institutional, and managerial factors are mentioned in the literature as relevant to the actual use of information systems.

According to a study conducted in different ministries in Kenya, development bureaucracies are not naturally supportive of the use of information systems for analysis and policy-making, due to such factors as their administrative cultures, the nature of bureaucratic work, the skills of personnel, and their prevailing organisational structure.[24]

According to a study on the adoption of computerised information systems in the public sector in Kenya and Indonesia, the support from the local political leadership is critical to the effective introduction of new tools for information-handling. When this support is contradictory – as was the case in Bahia – the result is a 'considerable confusion on the part of the professional staff regarding the real value of the microcomputers, and more resistance to learning to use them'.[25] Strong external pressures are necessary to overcome this situation. Moreover, the new tools for information-handling must 'meet a fairly explicit perceived need for change, rather than a vague expectation of general improvement'.[26] On-the-job training is crucial to the effective use of the new information system, and it is particularly effective when there is actual responsiveness to the users' needs. The presence of external, credible advisors is recognised to be a key factor for the actual use of the available information for policy-making and for obtaining impact on decision-making.[27]

It is suggested that these advisors act in a collaborative and open way, to promote initiative and creativity among the staff.[28] When information systems for planning are introduced top-down and users are locked into rigid and non-responsive systems, the likely result is a failure – as a case study at the district level from India seems to suggest.[29]

The importance of these factors for the information system use is basically confirmed by our case-study of Pau da Lima. The information system was eventually accepted and used by the health district management. Besides the quality of the technology employed, this was due to the following factors:

- support by external advisors (the project management);
- credibility and legitimacy which the advisors gradually gained;
- a constant interaction between them and the health district management;
- a concrete demand for tools supporting decision-making and the responsiveness of these tools to the users' needs;
- on-the-job training through a specific exercise of data analysis.

6.5 CONCLUSIONS

In Pau da Lima information acted as an incentive to specificity (or specificity surrogate) in decision-making. Clear priorities, targets and – to some extent – actions were defined in a complex environment. Knowledge-building dealt basically with the reduction of this complexity. However, the quality of decisions was not improved simply because of the availability of manageable information. Standard procedures had to be set for the use of an information system supported by a sophisticated technology. This simplified data analysis and put pressures on the decision-makers, stimulating the agreement on the targets and thus determining impact on decision-making. The process worked as displayed in Figure 6.1.

The *direct* influence of available data on decision-making was weak. Data obtained from different activities of knowledge-building (box one) only indirectly determined an improvement in the final product of decision-making (box six). Strong elements from the blueprint approach had to be injected into the decision-making process (boxes two, three, four, five) in order to increase the degree of specificity of the activities involved.

This is not to say, however, that the almost exclusive presence of elements from the blueprint approach can be responsible for better decisions. Political aspects of negotiation, consensus-building, and persuasion cannot be eliminated from decision-making processes. These elements, as we saw, were important in convincing the health district

FIGURE 6.1
DECISION-MAKING IN PAU DA LIMA

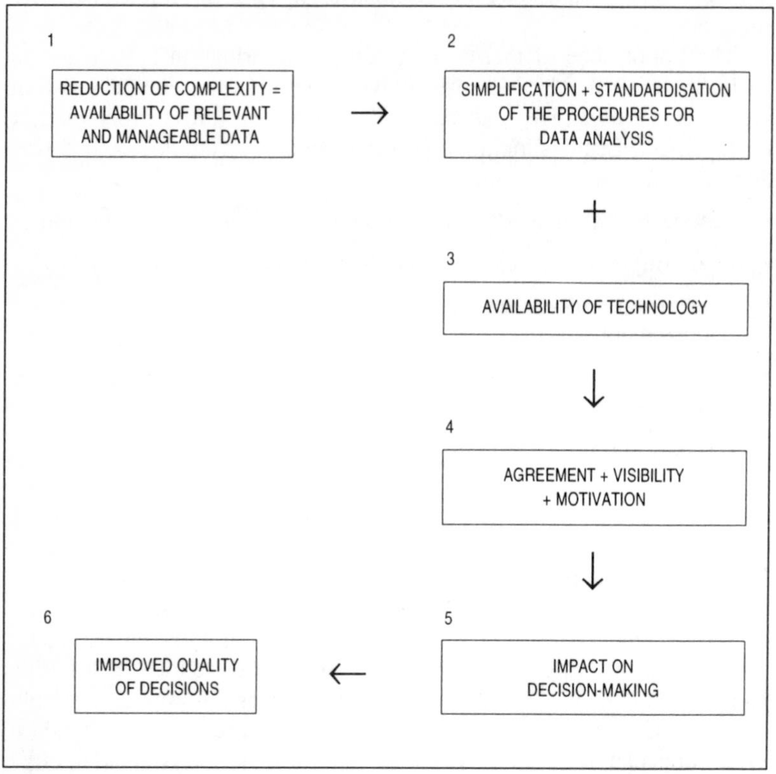

management to use the information system. Moreover, their presence was even more important at a decisional level higher than the health district: 'blueprinting' the decision-making process helped to make the possible alternatives clear – but in the end, political considerations became crucial to the final decision. The case of Cana Brava was a clear example in this respect. The decision at the municipal level to select this area for a $ 3.5 million sanitation programme was influenced by the data provided by the health district of Pau da Lima, as well as by the political visibility of the problems of Cana Brava itself.

NOTES

1. Distrito Sanitário Pau da Lima, *Plano Operativo do Distrito Sanitário de Pau da Lima* (Salvador, Brazil: mimeo, 1989).
2. We use the term 'exercise', as it was meant to test the actual functioning of the

information system and included aspects of on-the-job training. However, such an exercise was made with real data and for concrete purposes (selecting the micro-areas in which to concentrate actions for the prevention of diarrhoeal diseases). In this sense, it was an exercise but not a simulation.

3. In the previous chapter we saw that this variable had a low reliability in absolute terms, but a relatively good one in terms of ranking. Therefore, it was decided to use this indicator, on the assumption that it was able to identify at least the poorest areas of the health district – that is, those areas which were actually relevant for targeting.
4. Maps and tables are displayed, and the whole analytical procedure followed during the exercise is described, in the Technical Appendix C.
5. With regard to income, instead, no significant differences appeared between the micro-areas and the HCRAs.
6. According to Israel, the 'potential for specification' is one of the components of the concept of specificity. It coincides with the potential for defining with precision objectives, methods, and control systems. See A. Israel, *Institutional Development. Incentives to Performance* (Baltimore: Johns Hopkins University Press, 1987), p. 52. The other components of the concept of specificity seem to derive, to some extent, from such a potential. They refer to the intensity, timing, traceability and spread of the effects; the ways in which the motivation and behaviour of the participants is affected; and the type of actions undertaken by the latter in response to the effects, together with the way in which their job is interpreted.
7. A. Israel (1987), op. cit., p. 146.
8. A. Israel (1987), op. cit., pp. 179–83.
9. R. Heaver, *Adapting a Training and Visit Extension System for Family Planning, Health and Nutrition Programs* (Washington, DC: World Bank Staff Working Paper 662, 1984), p. ii.
10. According to Dangermond, '[b]y sharing a common data base, people with different perspectives, interests, training, and points of view can often be brought together to solve problems. [...] GIS may then provide one means for both seeing problems holistically and also for encouraging people to share the process of solving them.' J. Dangermond, 'Geographic Information System Technology and Development Planning', *Regional Development Dialogue*, 11, 3 (1990) pp. 6–7.
11. Statements by the health district manager and several PAHO officials, pronounced during the second meeting of evaluation of the HEAP project, Salvador, July 1993.
12. Although we have no systematic evidence in this respect, we can argue that actions at the micro-area level can be programmed as many small and different blueprints, tailor-made to the context of each micro-area, and oriented towards a common objective. Blueprint should be possible at the micro-area level, because – by definition – the micro-area is homogeneous, that is, variability and uncertainty that make the blueprint inadequate are reduced in it. This would ease the implementation of people-oriented actions at the grassroots level, by subjecting them to standard procedures typical of 'zipper' programmes. See R. Chambers, 'Bureaucratic Reversals and Local Diversity', *IDS Bulletin*, 19, 4 (1988a), p. 51
13. These data refer to general clinics, gynecology and pediatrics. Productivity is measured as the percentage of programmed medical consultations which had

been actually carried out in the year. The programmed consultations are calculated on the basis of the average number of consultations per doctor per day, multiplied by the number of doctors and working days in a year.

14. Although it would have been possible and easy to print, distribute, and discuss in the health centres some relevant maps and tables produced with the support of the GIS.
15. In this respect, Peterson argues that in LDCs, 'much of the computer technology is provided under technical assistance projects. [...] Donors often provide technical assistance staff to do the analysis of data. Such technical assistance often preempts analysis by ministry officers. Where at all possible, analysis should be done through a rigorous program of counterpart related training.' S.B. Peterson, *From Processing to Analyzing: Intensifying the Use of Microcomputers in Development Bureaucracies* (Cambridge, MA: Harvard Institute for International Development, Development Discussion Paper, 1990a), p. 31.
16. At present we know that the information system remains in routine use by the health district management of Pau da Lima. Rapid appraisal has been repeated once to update the original data, and epidemiological information is currently being collected in the health centres and stored in the information system. In July 1994 a PAHO consultancy was requested by the health district of Pau da Lima to develop the information system further, by introducing a more recent and powerful version of the geographic software.
17. J. Moris, *Managing Induced Rural Development* (Bloomington, IN: International Development Institute, 1981), p. 43.
18. C.E. Lindblom, 'The Sociology of Planning: Thought and Social Interaction', in M. Bornstein (ed.), *Economic Planning East and West* (Cambridge, MA: Ballinger Publishing Company, 1975), p. 39.
19. R. Chambers, *Managing Rural Development: Ideas and Experience from East Africa* (West Hartford, CT.: Kumarian Press, 1985), p. 116.
20. A. Israel (1987), op cit., p. 147.
21. H. Leibenstein, *Beyond Economic Man: a New Foundation for Micro-economics* (Cambridge, MA: Harvard University Press, 1976), Ch. 15.
22. A.O. Hirschman, *Development Projects Observed* (Washington, DC: Brookings Institutions, 1967).
23. A. Israel (1987), op. cit.
24. S.B. Peterson (1990a), p. 4.
25. J. Brodman, *Microcomputers Adoption in Developing Countries: Old Management Style and New Information Systems* (University of Maryland: International Management Development Centre, 1985), p. 136.
26. J. Brodman (1985), op.cit., p. 137.
27. J. Brodman (1985), op. cit., p. 147.
28. S.B. Peterson, 'Institutionalizing Microcomputers in Developing Bureaucracies: Theory and Practice from Kenya', *Information Technology for Development*, 5, 3 (1990b), p. 304.
29. S. Madon, 'Introducing Administrative Reform through the Application of Computer-based Information Systems: a Case-study from India', *Public Administration and Development*, 13 (1993), p. 45.

7
Conclusion

This study was elaborated on the basis of some assumptions. We argued that an appropriate mix of elements from the blueprint and the process approach respectively is necessary to manage people-oriented activities. Such a mix is intended to increase the degree of both flexibility and specificity of these activities. At the operational level it is important to achieve a 'fit' between knowledge-building about needs and decision-making for planning and management. We formulated also the hypothesis that information-handling represents a promising area for realising such a mix.

In our analysis of information-handling in Pau da Lima we saw that information generated at the community level was gradually transformed in order to become an effective incentive to specificity (or specificity surrogate) in decision-making. Certain tools proved to be particularly useful in this respect.

Rapid appraisal, participatory, and bottom-up methods of data collection are among these tools. A process, flexible approach was adopted to collect meaningful data on local needs – that is, to deal with people who had to express their own needs. Open questionnaires were employed to let respondents express their subjective demands, and a flexible research design was used to cover a differentiated range of social points of view on these needs and to perceive local diversity. Social interaction – a basic hallmark of the process approach – was central to the whole procedure. By fostering a high degree of social interaction between the project and the community, the perception of local reality of the outsiders (the project) could be integrated with that of the insiders (the community) – thus controlling the anti-poor bias which is often implicit in the former.[1]

With regard to the appropriateness of the application of these procedures, we tend to argue that the use of bottom-up, rapid appraisal procedures is a crucial and often necessary instrument to collect relevant data on those areas which are reached with difficulty by the official statistics – as is usually the case for heterogeneous, sub-urban areas in large cities in LDCs.

However, we saw also that these methods alone cannot support effectively the decision-making processes necessary to manage complex organisations or projects. For that, information so generated has to pass through a further analytic treatment performed by professionals – which usually involves the application of blueprint elements.

In Pau da Lima, we saw that a more balanced approach was adopted in data processing. Data on needs were systematised, standardised, and computerised in order to render them manageable and more precise. Elements of the process approach were still present in the gradual definition of the micro-areas, the holistic way in which these were considered, and the information system design. However, these were balanced by elements of the blueprint approach, such as the analytic devices and the systematic procedures used to systematise and standardise the data, and the technical requirements imposed by data computerisation.

As a result, the territory of the health district was divided into micro-areas. We saw that these are quite reliable as well as valid categories – they express in a manageable and specific way differences in living conditions, which are relevant for health district management.

In Pau da Lima, the interpretation of a heterogeneous territory was a complex task. The territory was gradually broken down into meaningful component parts or units of analysis (the micro-areas), which were then analysed in-depth. In this sense, the whole process of knowledge-building could be seen as an effort aimed at reducing the complexity of a composite territory, in order to make it more comprehensible. Elements from the process approach were used when the project had to deal with complexity – to embrace heterogeneous and subjective points of view about needs. But elements from the blueprint approach were used when the moment came to reduce this complexity, as aspects of analysis and decision-making became central to the project – that is, when this moved from the community to the management level.

The micro-areas can be considered useful specificity surrogates. Also in this case, their applicability seems to be appropriate to urban heterogeneous areas – no evidence is available for other types of areas (for instance urban and homogeneous, or rural with a scattered population).

In decision-making the elements of the process approach – and, consequently, flexibility – were reduced. A minimal discretion was left to decision-makers for choosing between the different options offered by the information system. Data analysis was guided by standardised, blueprint procedures, aimed at increasing the visibility of local problems, and promoting agreement and motivation among decision-makers. The result was an improvement in the quality of decisions – very precise targets could be prioritised, and tailor-made actions programmed for some of the selected micro-areas.

The sensitive use of a GIS proved to be quite fruitful in this respect. In a GIS all data are referred to specific geographic locations – geographic categories are clear-cut, well delimited and manageable, and several different data can be ascribed to them at the same time. We tend to argue that GISs too are potentially useful specificity surrogates – although, in our case-study, we saw that only small geographic categories used to refer the available information are highly precise ones.

Different devices for information-handling were used with success in the Pau da Lima project. Before concluding our study, we can try to single out some of the conditions which were necessary for their successful adoption and use.

A first condition for the successful development of new tools for information-handling was their simplicity. Simple instruments were used in knowledge-building – such as a geographic grid, or tables of comparisons between micro-areas. Their use required professional but not sophisticated skills, together with a certain degree of methodological self-consciousness. Simplicity and user-friendliness were also basic guidelines for the information system design. Finally, a simplified process of data crossing was made possible by means of a codified interface for the use of the information system. In this respect, Chambers' plea in favour of 'a new rigour based on the two principles of optimal ignorance – knowing what it is worth not knowing – and proportionate accuracy – recognising the degree of accuracy required'[2] was basically satisfied.

A second condition refers to the presence of external resources, provided by the Italian technical assistance and PAHO. These provided the health district of Pau da Lima with the funds necessary to implement the rapid appraisal survey, to purchase the hardware and software, and to develop the specific GIS application. More generally, they provided the health district of Pau da Lima with technical co-operation to experiment with an innovative approach to information-handling. In an unfavourable context such as that of Bahia, the existence of technical co-operation projects was certainly crucial for the institutional development of the health district of Pau da Lima. In more favourable contexts fewer external resources would be necessary to replicate the experience of Pau da Lima.[3]

However, the way in which the project was managed was also important. This was managed in a flexible, gradual, and incremental way. The different methods and tools for data collection and data processing had not been pre-established at the beginning of the project – rather, they were developed during the project's implementation, as responses to emerging obstacles and opportunities. The information system was also designed and programmed in a gradual way and in close interaction with its future users.

In addition, the project of Pau da Lima was managed in a collaborative way. This allowed a high degree of interaction between the project's staff and the local partners. This interaction, together with traditional managerial tools such as training and supervision, stimulated the commitment and motivation of the local partners, and fostered consensus relationships within the project team.

Commitment, motivation and consensus were necessary conditions especially for the use of the new information system by the health district management. These conditions could be satisfied only when the project management gained sufficient legitimacy and a concrete demand was made on the part of the health district management for a tool in support of decision-making.

The need for these conditions to be satisfied calls for a final comment. From our case-study, we can argue that specificity surrogates are not accepted and used merely because 'they work' in a technical sense. They are managerial tools, and as such, they do not exist in a vacuum – instead, their applicability is always limited to a given organisational context. It is not worth, then, concentrating efforts only on their technical improvement, without paying due attention to their institutional and social convenience. In Pau da Lima certain tools for information-handling worked because they were developed from within the project rather than imposed top-down, as well as with flexibility, incrementalism, and in a collaborative way. This process was a long and difficult one, but nonetheless crucial to the success of the project.

This suggests that, no matter how good managerial surrogates to specificity can be, it will always be necessary to experiment, in the practice of the projects and through trial-and-error, with new ones or the adaptation of those which already exist. Our hope is that this study has provided a modest, but nonetheless useful contribution in this respect.

NOTES

1. On the relationship between 'outsiders' and 'insiders' in project management, see R. Chambers, *Rural Development: Putting the Last First* (London: Longman, 1983).
2. R. Chambers, 'Rapid Rural Appraisal: Rationale and Repertoire', *Public Administration and Development*, 1 (1981), p. 95.
3. The same methodologies and tools for information-handling which were developed in Pau da Lima were successfully implemented in other Brazilian cities, where slightly different conditions had to be satisfied. The most interesting is the case of São Paulo, where an information system was implemented in two large health districts. The local context of São Paulo was more favourable than that of Bahia. The support by the municipal secretariat of health to the implementation of health districts was generally effective; the health districts were legally formalised administrative entities, with a budget of their own; and considerable local technical as well as financial resources were available. Here, the expatriate team could work in a purely advisory role. The same process which took place in Pau da Lima was implemented with fewer external resources and with a much lighter role for the expatriate staff.

Technical Appendix A
Data Collection

DATA BASES AND MAPS INCLUDED IN THE INFORMATION SYSTEM OF PAU DA LIMA

Tables A.1 and A.2 illustrate, in a synthetic way, for each data base and each map: the information included, the techniques of data generation which have been used, and the predominant type of data (primary or secondary).

TABLE A.1

MAPS INCLUDED IN THE INFORMATION SYSTEM IN PAU DA LIMA

MAPS	DATA INCLUDED	METHODS OF DATA COLLECTION	TYPE OF DATA
Boundaries of the health district	Administrative boundaries	The boundaries are set by the central level	Secondary
Boundaries of the HCRAs	Geographic barriers	Rapid Appraisal	Primary
Boundaries of the micro-areas	Socio-economic and environmental	Rapid Appraisal	Primary
Roads	Name of the roads, numbers delimiting blocks	Existing maps + mapping in the field	Primary and secondary
Streams, health centres, schools, local associations	Name and localisation	Existing maps + mapping in the field	Primary and secondary

TABLE A.2

DATA BASES INCLUDED IN THE INFORMATION SYSTEM IN PAU DA LIMA

DATA BASES	DATA INCLUDED	METHODS OF DATA COLLECTION	TYPE OF DATA
Health centre	Characteristics of the health centre (human resources, opening hours etc.), localisation of the clientele, productivity of services, morbidity, access	Health centre's records	Secondary
Patients registered in the health centres	Number of the personal clinical record, name, address, sex, age, job	Registration form	Secondary
Transmittable diseases of compulsory notification	Health centre, epidemiological week, disease, name, sex, age, address	Health centre's records (weekly bulletin of compulsory notification)	Secondary
Deaths	Name, date of death, civil status, sex, age, place of death, address, job, if the patient received medical care, cause of death	Survey on death certificates, stored by SESAB	Secondary
Socio-economic and environmental data for HCRAs	Area, quantitative scores for several characteristics of the area: inhabitants, productive activities, number of health centres, pharmacies and schools, transport, housing conditions, water and sanitation, garbage disposal, average family income, basic consumption	Rapid Appraisal and estimates from official sources for demographic data	Primary and some secondary
Socio-economic, environmental data for micro-areas	The same as for the HCRAs (description and scores), plus: demographic density, more common jobs.	Rapid Appraisal and estimates from official sources for demographic data	Primary and some secondary

DESCRIPTION OF PRIMARY DATA COLLECTION

Items included in the rapid appraisal questionnaire

Physical environment: topography, presence of geophysical risks.

Existing infrastructure: housing, water and sanitation conditions, garbage removal, transport, electricity, presence of schools, pharmacies, shops and supermarkets, other public services.

Socio-economic situation: average educational level, average family income level, most frequent jobs.

Health conditions: most frequent diseases according to the local population's perception.

Use of local health services: health services most frequently used and main problems in their functioning.

Existing local associations and their achievements.

Personnel Employed for Fieldwork and their Requested Characteristics

Nine students from the local faculties of sociology and economics were selected and received a one-week theoretical and practical training on rapid appraisal methods. Fieldworkers had to have a capacity for self-planning, a good methodological background and awareness of the importance of methodology, reasonable analytical skills, and a propensity for team-work. Unskilled personnel were not thought to be suitable for fieldwork, as this implied an active role by interviewers, who were supposed to take decisions during their daily activities with regard to the interviewees' selection and the identification of each interview's focus.

Procedures for the Execution of Fieldwork

Fieldworkers were provided with questionnaires and a map of each *bairro*, which had to be gradually filled in. Interviews and systematic observations of the area occurred simultaneously and were reciprocally supportive. Each bit of information – from both interviews and observations – had to be referred to a geographic location on the map. Fieldwork usually started in each *bairro* with a systematic reconnaissance visit. The initial interviews began with questions aimed at obtaining a provisional division of the area into different settlements. The questions were then referred to this provisional territorial division, to assess if differences actually existed between the sub-areas which had been identified so far, with regard to the different items of the questionnaire (housing conditions, water and sanitation, income level and so on). In this way, an initial and still provisional 'geographic grid' was constructed, which was then used as a guide to orient further fieldwork. The interviewers were then gradually concentrated in the sub-areas for which a clear picture had not yet emerged, while the questions were narrowed down to the items for which doubts still existed. The grid was then progressively filled in and modified until a satisfactory picture of the whole *bairro* emerged.

Demographic Data

A mixture of methods was used for the collection of demographic data, as well as a mixture of both primary and secondary sources; nevertheless, when doubts arose, the ultimate test was provided by data collected in the field – therefore, we consider demographic data as mainly primary data.

Different sources were used, namely: existing data for the new buildings constructed by the government; aerial photographs, which were compared with the existing maps, in order to assess the actual expansion of the urbanised areas in Pau da Lima; regularly updated maps drawn by the Federal Agency for the Control of Malaria (SUCAM); estimates done by the National Institute of Geography and Statistics (IBGE) on the number of dwellings in the city of Salvador, which had been used to organise the 1991 census.

However, when no other data were available, or when doubts could not be solved by cross-checking between different secondary data, fieldworkers were sent into the new settlements in order to draw detailed maps, indicating each single dwelling of each area. An architect was contracted to draw the maps.

From all these data, a final estimate of the population of Pau da Lima was obtained. According to this estimate, Pau da Lima had, at the beginning of 1992, about 150,000 inhabitants. This global figure was then disaggregated into data for, respectively, each health centre's responsibility area, and each micro-area.

Maps

The procedures adopted to update and complete the existing maps were basically the same which had been used to estimate the population of Pau da Lima. Aerial pictures, maps by SUCAM and observation in the field were used to draw the maps of recent settlements. The observation was useful also to indicate and verify the names of the new streets, as well as the numbers of the dwellings respectively at the beginning and the end of each block of these streets. These indications were crucial in plotting the epidemiological events and other data on the map by means of a GIS.

The boundaries of the health centres' responsibility areas were drawn by considering the presence of geographic barriers which could limit the access of residents of certain areas to the health centres. Data on geographic barriers – waterways, large roads, hills, steep valleys and so on – were collected by fieldworkers during the rapid appraisal survey.

The boundaries of the micro-areas were drawn by considering the geographic distribution of different values of the socio-economic and environmental variables which had been investigated during the rapid appraisal.

ASSESSMENT OF THE PERFORMANCE OF RAPID APPRAISAL METHODS

Coverage

TABLE A.3

TYPES OF KEY INFORMANTS INTERVIEWED IN PAU DA LIMA

TYPE OF INFORMANT	NUMBER	PERCENTAGE
Leaders of local associations	31	35.6
Old residents	20	23.0
Teachers	18	20.7
Personnel of the health centres	11	12.7
Traders and shopkeepers	7	8.0
TOTAL	**87**	**100**

(*Source*: rapid appraisal questionnaires)

From the analysis of Table A.3 we notice that key informants from the 'community' as a whole (local leaders, old residents, traders and shopkeepers) represent 66.6 per cent of all the respondents, whilst 33.4 per cent of interviewees are members of institutions (teachers and personnel of the health centres).

Locational Precision

Data could be made locationally precise by key informants in either of two ways: (i) by referring to the *bairro* as a whole, but providing clear indications on the *bairro*'s internal differentiation, or (ii) by referring to specific locations within the *bairro* itself (in this case, data could be subsequently assembled to build up a picture of the *bairro* as a whole).

The answers to the questionnaires were analysed in order to assess to what extent respondents succeeded in differentiating and/or localising the information they provided. Two sets of questionnaires only were considered in-depth – those referring to the *bairros* of Dom Avelar and Pau da Lima. Pau da Lima (94,000 inhabitants) and Dom Avelar (11,000 inhabitants) are representative of two different types of *bairros*, the former being large and heterogeneous, and the latter small and more homogeneous.

We have classified the answers to the questionnaires according to their territorial reference, by using the following codes:

(a) reference to the *bairro* as a whole, without differentiation (not locationally precise answer).

(b) reference to the *bairro* as a whole, but with indications about its internal differentiation (locationally precise answer);

(c) reference to a specific sub-area of the *bairro* – usually the sub-area where the informant resides and/or works (locationally precise answer).

In order to make the analysis more manageable, just nine items of the questionnaire have been chosen: three items referring to the infrastructure and environmental situation (housing conditions, water availability and sanitation); three referring to the socio-economic situation (education, income, and most frequent jobs); one referring to health perception (most diffused diseases); one referring to the use by residents of existing local health services; and one referring to the knowledge by the respondents of the existence of local associations.

Twelve questionnaires were filled in Dom Avelar and 24 in Pau da Lima. As nine items have been considered from each questionnaire, we have therefore analysed 108 answers from Dom Avelar and 218 from Pau da Lima.

A careful analysis of the text of each answer for each selected item has been done. Empirically, the answers have been classified according to explicit territorial references which could be found in the text. The results are reported in Table A.4.

In both *bairros*, slightly less than half of the answers are locationally precise, as they differentiate and/or localise their information: if we sum up the percentages of answers classified as (b) and (c) we obtain, respectively for the *bairros* considered, 42 and 48 per cent of all the answers.

Nevertheless, when we consider each type of answer, those classified as (a) are the most frequent – 32 per cent in both Pau da Lima and Dom Avelar. These are not locationally precise answers.

TABLE A.4

CLASSIFICATION OF THE ANSWERS TO THE QUESTIONNAIRES ACCORDING TO THEIR TERRITORIAL REFERENCE

	CODES				
BAIRRO	(a) not locationally precise	(b) locationally precise	(c) locationally precise	n.a.	TOTAL
Pau da Lima%	32	18	24	26	100
(N°)	(69)	(39)	(52)	(56)	(216)
Dom Avelar %	32	29	19	20	100
(N°)	(35)	(31)	(20)	(22)	(108)

n.a. = not available (answers were lacking or could not be classified)
(*Source*: rapid appraisal questionnaires)

We analysed further the available data in order to assess the degree of locational precision of each item of the questionnaire.[1] The main results of the analysis can be summarised as follows:

- The answers classified as (a) tend to be concentrated in three items: 'education', 'most frequent diseases' and 'health centres used'. In fact, in Dom Avelar 60, 100 and 90 per cent of valid answers respectively (that is, excluding non-available answers) for these items are classified as locationally not precise; the same figures for Pau da Lima are, respectively, 73, 95 and 79 per cent.
- In contrast, items like 'housing', 'sanitation', and – to a lesser extent – 'jobs' and 'water' perform well with regard to the capacity, by key informants, to provide differentiated and/or well-localised information. By aggregating the answers of types (b) and (c), in fact, 'housing' obtains a percentage of 91 and 100 of all valid answers respectively in Dom Avelar and Pau da Lima; the figures for 'sanitation' are 100 and 83 per cent respectively in the two *bairros*; 'jobs' obtains 89 per cent in Dom Avelar and 58 per cent in Pau da Lima, and 'water' respectively 64 and 63 per cent.

Finally, we analysed the capacity, by different types of key informants, to provide locationally precise information. When we considered the answers of types (b) and (c) only, that is, 'differentiated' and 'localised' answers, we could see that:

- The personnel from the health centres always 'differentiate' (100 per cent of their answers are of type 'b' in both Pau da Lima and Dom Avelar).

- In contrast, ordinary people (old residents) most frequently tend to 'localise' (97 and 70 per cent of their answers are of type 'c' respectively in the two *bairros*).
- Local leaders, finally, tend to provide answers of both types in a well-balanced way (54 per cent of type 'b' and 46 per cent of type 'c' answers in Pau da Lima, and respectively 48 and 52 per cent respectively in Dom Avelar).

The answers provided by both teachers and traders/shopkeepers are too erratic to be interpreted in any meaningful way.

DESCRIPTION OF SECONDARY DATA COLLECTION

For each patient who registered in the health centres, a registration form was prepared which included the following data: health centre, date, number of registration, name, sex, age, job and address of the patient. A very detailed manual with instructions on the procedures to follow was prepared and distributed to the health centres. The clerks who worked in the latter were responsible for all the registration procedures of the patients. When a patient went to the health centre, the clerk had to fill in the registration form (two copies), and give the patient an identity card with his/her number of registration. One copy of the registration forms was stored in the health centre, in alphabetic order. The other copy was sent to the health district management, and digitised into a data base. The digitised data were then checked by a clerk of the health district, who had been previously trained.

When a patient went to the health centre for health care, the attending doctor had to fill in a single form, which included the following data: registration number of the patient, date, reason for the request for medical care, diagnosis, result of the consultation (treated/referred to a specialist/further consultation requested). All these data were then copied onto the patient's clinical record, which was stored in the health centre under the patient's registration number. When a patient went to the health centre, the clerk had simply to search for his/her clinical record, by the registration number.

The same single form filled in by the doctor was used to produce data on the diseases of compulsory notification. These included the transmittable diseases to be notified by law (diseases which can be prevented by means of immunisation, sexually transmittable diseases, meningitis, TB, leptospirosis, hepatitis), as well as the diseases which were known as the most frequent in the health district of Pau da Lima (diarrhoeal diseases, acute respiratory infections, scabies).

When the occurrence of these diseases was detected in a patient, the patient's data were reported, together with the indication of the disease, in a weekly bulletin of compulsory notification, which each health centre's director had to send to the member of the health district management team responsible for epidemiological surveillance. These data were digitised into a data base.

NOTE

1. This test was not possible for those items which showed a high percentage of non-available answers.

Technical Appendix B
Data Processing

THE ATTRIBUTION OF SCORES

An example can be useful to clarify the procedure for the attribution of scores. We consider the item of 'water'. For this item, the following situations could be found in the district, according to the *bairros* reports:

- legal connection with the water system/regular provision of water;
- legal connection with the water system/irregular provision of water;
- illegal connections with the water system;
- use of springs, wells, fountains, rivers.

Different combinations of these situations were found in different micro-areas. The frequency of these combinations as well as their respective degree of risk for the health of the resident population were analysed. It was observed that the irregular provision of water obliged residents to store the water in tanks, hence exposing it to pollution. Illegal connections represented a similar risk, as water could be contaminated because of bad junctions. Such a risk was increased when springs, wells and fountains were also used. However, as rivers often receive untreated sewage, they are usually more polluted than springs, wells and fountains. Therefore, the use of water from rivers represented a higher risk than that from springs, wells and fountains.

Then the following scores were attributed to the item of water:

- score one (minimum risk): legal connection with the water system/regular provision;

- score two (low risk): legal connection with the water system/irregular provision and/or illegal connections;
- score three (medium risk): illegal connections and/or use of springs, wells and fountains;
- score four (maximum risk): illegal connections and/or use of springs, wells, fountains as well as rivers.

Similar typologies were prepared for other items, such as sanitation, housing conditions, and so on. For those items which were already expressed in quantitative terms (such as income), the attribution of scores was almost automatic.

ASSESSMENT OF PRIMARY DATA PROCESSING

Data from the rapid appraisal and from the household survey referred to three micro-areas. These were the micro-areas of the 'Conjunto Sete de Abril' (a group of housing developments built by the government for middle-class families), the 'Loteamento Jardim Nova Esperança' (a spontaneous, but legal settlement) and the 'Invasão Castelo Branco' (a group of slums or *favelas*, where house-ownership was not legally recognised).

The household survey was conducted in the following way: in each micro-area – whose number of inhabitants was similar – a sample of about ten per cent of the resident families was randomly chosen, by selecting one dwelling out of ten on the maps. In total, 80 questionnaires were used in each micro-area. The rate of response was quite high – 92 per cent of the questionnaires were filled in (221 out of 240). Data were collected in the field in October and November of 1990, one year later than data collection through rapid appraisal methods. As the items which were compared do not usually show dramatic changes within one year, the comparison was considered as legitimate.

The following items were considered for the comparison between household survey data and rapid appraisal data: housing conditions, water, sanitation, level of family income, most frequent jobs. These items are the most relevant from among those which were actually used for the division of the territory of Pau da Lima into micro-areas. Housing conditions, water and sanitation usually represent the most dangerous environmental risks, whilst income and jobs are generally accepted as valid indicators of living conditions at large – they reflect respectively the purchasing power of a family and its position within the wider productive structure.

The analysis of data collected through the household survey yielded tables such as Table B.1. This had to be compared with Table B.2, containing information obtained through rapid appraisal methods and disaggregated at the micro-area level.

In Table B.1, housing conditions are classified as precarious (wood and plastic), semi-precarious (mud and straw) and permanent (bricks). The item of water includes the following situations: legal connections to the water system, illegal connections to the water system, use of wells, springs, fountains, rivers, and use of water from a neighbour who is connected (usually illegally) to the water system. Sanitation distinguishes the following cases: connection to the sewage system, individual pit, collective pit (that is, for a number of dwellings), latrine, existence of uncovered drainage channels used for sewage, use of open-air disposal (i.e. open spaces with no infrastructure) near home. Income levels (expressed in minimum salaries per month)[1] are classified in a very disaggregated way from half a minimum salary to five, then in an aggregated way from five to ten and finally above ten. Job is classified into the following categories: permanently employed (for both employees and self-employed), retired, domestic work (maid, washer, home-cleaner, cook, and so on but regularly and permanently employed), informal work (any working activity not permanent and/or performed without a formal working permit), unemployed. For all items, not available (n.a.) answers are reported. Quantitative data are expressed as percentages for each micro-area.

Reliability

In all the micro-areas data about housing conditions and water are basically coincident. Data about jobs seem to coincide too with regard to the basic distinction between formal and informal workers. In Sete de Abril only retired people were not detected by rapid appraisal methods; as they receive a regular income, they were probably confused by key informants with the mass of the employed.

In the micro-area of Sete de Abril, data coincide with respect to sanitation too, as all dwellings are provided with some type of sanitation of their own. However, rapid appraisal data are more complete, as risks for a micro-area nearby are detected.

The situation of sanitation is not immediately clear in Jardim Nova Esperança: according to survey data almost 90 per cent of houses are provided with a reasonable form of sanitation (individual or collective pits): apparently no risks are generated by the lack of sanitation in the area. However, the existence of open-air drainage channels was detected through rapid appraisal methods in parts of the micro-area. The presence of these open-air drainage channels is due to the rudimentary way in which the pits were dug: the area of Jardim Nova Esperança grew up

TABLE B.1
CHARACTERISTICS OF THREE MICRO-AREAS – HOUSEHOLD SURVEY (PERCENTAGES FOR EACH MICRO-AREA)

ITEM	CONJ. SETE DE ABRIL	JARDIM NOVA ESPERANÇA	INV. CASTELO BRANCO
HOUSING			
Precarious	0	1.25	29.0
Semi-precarious	0	0	34.0
Permanent	92.5	96.2	29.0
n.a.	7.5	2.55	8.0
TOTAL	100.0	100.0	100.0
WATER			
Legal connection	91.25	91.25	36.7
Illegal connection	0	5.0	39.2
Well	0	0	2.5
Spring	0	0	3.8
Fountain	0	0	0
River	0	0	0
Neighbour	1.25	1.25	8.8
n.a.	7.5	2.5	9.0
TOTAL	100.0	100.0	100.0
SANITATION			
Connection to the sewage system	63.7	0	2.5
Individual pit	25.0	75.0	27.8
Collective pit	1.25	13.7	2.5
Latrine	0	0	0
Open-air drainage	0	3.75	18.9
Open-air disposal	0	0	30.3
Other forms of sanitation	0	3.75	8.3
n.a.	10.05	3.8	9.7
TOTAL	100.0	100.0	100.0
INCOME			
Up to 0.5 min. salaries	0	3.7	5.0
From 0.5 to 1 min. salaries	12.5	10.0	10.1
From 1 to 2 min. salaries	5.0	20.0	29.1
From 2 to 3 min. salaries	10.0	6.2	22.7
From 3 to 4 min. salaries	0	0	0
From 4 to 5 min. salaries	23.7	23.7	13.9
From 5 to 10 min. salaries	23.7	22.5	11.3
More than 10 min. salaries	15.0	5.0	0
n.a.	10.1	8.9	7.9
TOTAL	100.0	100.0	100.0
JOB			
Employed	41.25	62.5	51.8
Retired	27.5	7.5	0
Domestic work	6.25	3.9	0
Informal	13.75	22.5	36.7
Unemployed	2.5	1.33	3.8
n.a.	8.75	2.27	7.7
TOTAL	100.0	100.0	100.0

TABLE B.2
CHARACTERISTICS OF THREE MICRO-AREAS – RAPID APPRAISAL DATA

ITEMS	CONJUNTO SETE DE ABRIL	JARDIM NOVA ESPERANÇA	INVASÃO CASTELO BRANCO
HOUSING	100% permanent	100% permanent	25% precarious 40% semi-precarious 35% permanent
(score)	(1)	(1)	(3)
WATER	connected, irregular	connected, irregular; some illegal connections	older slums: connected, irregular; recent slums: illegal connections, wells, springs
(score)	(2)	(2)	(3)
SANITATION	flats are connected to boxes that throw untreated waters on slums nearby	some sanitation in the main streets; open-air drainage channels in the rest	limited sanitation; many dwellings use open-air drainage channels
(score)	(1)	(3)	(4)
INCOME	5–7 min. salaries	3–4 min. salaries	1–2 min. salaries
(score)	(1)	(2)	(3)
JOBS (This item was not ranked into scores)	civil servants, workers in petro-chemical industry; some shopkeepers; few informal workers	lower level civil servants; shopkeepers; some informal workers	lower level civil servants; employees; many informal workers: men in civil construction, women in domestic work for better-off families

spontaneously, residents gradually built up their houses and provided them with minimum infrastructure with no technical supervision; consequently, no efficient systems were built to discharge the pits, which tended to flood – especially during the rainy season – and to create open-air drainage channels in most of the area. Therefore, there was an effective lack of sanitation in Jardim Nova Esperança, which represented a risk for the local residents. Probably this risk would have been masked by focusing only on the individual characteristics of each household; instead, by looking at the area as a whole, the risk was detected. In this respect, rapid appraisal methods turned out to be more reliable than survey methods.

Survey data on sanitation also coincide broadly with rapid appraisal data in Castelo Branco: only one-third of the dwellings are provided with some form of sanitation (connections with the sewage system and/or pits), whilst almost two-thirds of them make use directly of open-air drainage channels, open-air disposals, or other risky forms of discharge.

Data about income, to the contrary, never coincide. In Sete de Abril, according to rapid appraisal data, the average income level of the micro-area is five to seven minimum salaries; according to survey data less than a quarter (23.7 per cent) of the resident families earn a similar income level (more than five and less than ten minimum salaries). Moreover, more than a quarter of the resident families (27.5 per cent) earn less than three minimum salaries and are not detected by rapid appraisal data. In Jardim Nova Esperança, according to rapid appraisal data the average income is three to four minimum salaries but according to survey data no families earn such an income. In Castelo Branco rapid appraisal data indicate an average income level of one to two minimum salaries; according to survey data only around 30 per cent of the resident families have such an income level; almost one quarter earn three minimum salaries and another quarter four minimum salaries or more, whilst five per cent earn half a minimum salary

Validity

The description of the characteristics of the three micro-areas which is reported in Table B.2 indicates a general, progressive deterioration of living conditions, from Sete de Abril to Jardim Nova Esperança, and from this to Castelo Branco.

Housing conditions are similar in Sete de Abril and Jardim Nova Esperança (score one in both), but worse in Castelo Branco (score three). The access to safe water is progressively more limited, as we consider the three micro-areas in turn. However, the threshold in terms of risk can be found in Castelo Branco (score three): notwithstanding their internal differences, the degree of risk is similar in Sete de Abril and Jardim Nova Esperança (score two in both). Sanitation is reasonable in the first micro-area (score one), but quite limited in the second one (score three), and very bad in the third one (score four). Levels of income are decreasing too, as we move from Sete de Abril (score one) to Jardim Nova Esperança (score two), and then to Castelo Branco (score three).

Finally, the proportion of regularly employed workers decreases, and the proportion of informal workers increases, when we compare Sete de Abril to Jardim Nova Esperança, and this to Castelo Branco.

When we compare these results to those from Table B.1, we find an immediate confirmation for housing and water. With regard to jobs there is a gradual increase in the percentage of informal workers. However, the items of sanitation and income deserve a deeper analysis, because they show a higher variability.

In Sete de Abril the situation of sanitation is not very variable: almost 90 per cent of the residents are provided with reasonable forms of sanitation, the majority of them (63.7 per cent) with the safest, and just a tiny minority uses collective pits; residents of this micro-area are hardly exposed to risks from the lack of sanitation.

In Jardim Nova Esperança the variability of sanitation is slightly higher: three-quarters of the residents have individual pits, almost 14 per cent have collective pits, and 7.5 per cent lack any form of sanitation at all. Despite this internal differentiation, the differences between this and the situation at Sete de Abril are clear: as no dwellings are connected to the sewage system, a relative level of risk is present for the micro-area as a whole – more clearly, at least 7.5 per cent of residents are definitely at risk because of the use of open-air drainage or disposal.

In Castelo Branco the internal variability of sanitation is high: almost one-third of the resident families use pits, an equal percentage use open-air disposals and about one-fifth use open-air drainage channels, whilst 8.3 per cent use other forms of disposal. However, the differences internal to this micro-area are less relevant than the differences with the other micro-areas: if we consider those who use open-air drainage channels, open-air disposal and other forms of disposal, we shall see that more than half (57.5 per cent) of the population of Castelo Branco are directly exposed to health risks from the lack of sanitation – a much higher percentage than those we saw in the other two micro-areas.

The validity of the division into micro-areas is confirmed, as both household survey data and rapid appraisal data indicate that relevant differences exist between the micro-areas with regard to the exposure to health risks due to the lack of sanitation.

We proceed now to analyse survey data about income. We group income levels into three broad classes:[2]

- zero to three minimum salaries (below the poverty line)
- four to ten minimum salaries (above the poverty line)
- more than ten minimum salaries (relative well-being)

We obtain Table B.3.

TABLE B.3

INCOME LEVELS FOR THREE SELECTED MICRO-AREAS, ACCORDING TO HOUSEHOLD SURVEY DATA (PERCENTAGES)

Minimum Salary	Sete de Abril	Jd. Nova Esperança	Castelo Branco
0–4	27.5	39.9	66.9
5–10	47.4	46.2	25.2
+10	15.0	5.0	0
n.a.	10.1	8.9	7.9
TOT	100	100	100

All the micro-areas show an internal variability – all classes are present in all micro-areas, except the class of more than ten minimum salaries in Castelo Branco. However, in this case too the differences between micro-areas are more striking than the differences within each micro-area. In both Sete de Abril and Jardim Nova Esperança class five–ten shows the highest frequency – almost half the population lives above the poverty line. Nevertheless, in Jardim Nova Esperança almost 40 per cent of the population live below the poverty line, and only five per cent are relatively well-off. The differences in living conditions are more striking in Castelo Branco, where the large majority of the population lives below the poverty line, and no families exist without problems related to satisfaction of their basic needs (more than ten minimum salaries).

We also notice that in all the micro-areas, income data provided by key informants are *always* underestimated, that is, there is a constant bias. This bias seems to increase when the general picture of a micro-area worsens. This is clear if we consider the average income level of every micro-area according to survey data, and compare it with rapid appraisal data: in Sete de Abril, the average shown in the survey data is 6.4 minimum salaries (rapid appraisal data: 5–7 minimum salaries); in Jardim Nova Esperança this is 5.2 minimum salaries (rapid appraisal data: 3–4 minimum salaries); and in Castelo Branco, 3.5 minimum salaries (rapid appraisal data: 1–2 minimum salaries)

This seems to indicate that rapid appraisal data on income, although hardly reliable in terms of absolute values, are quite reliable in terms of ranking. Therefore, also with regard to income, the division into micro-areas seems to be correct, as relevant differences among the micro-areas themselves are actually detected by rapid appraisal data.

Appendix B: Data Processing

DATA COMPUTERISATION

The geographic software package used in Pau da Lima was Mapinfo 5.01 for DOS, which included a DBMS in Foxbase. The hardware included: a Brazilian-made IBM-compatible 20 MHz AT-386 microcomputer with two megabyte RAM and eight megabyte hard disk, and colour monitor; a laser printer for high-quality output; and a digitiser for drawing the maps. The cost of the software and hardware did not exceed $5000 – a limited cost was obviously considered as crucial by the project management, in order to facilitate the replicability of the system. The system was developed by an expatriate computer engineer, who worked together with the project's epidemiologist and sociologist, and the health district management staff. The maps were digitised by a computer operator. Digitising is a time-consuming activity: it took about one month to digitise the whole health district (about 10,000 road segments). However, once the map of the health district was digitised, it was quite easy and fast to update it.[3]

NOTES

1. The value of the minimum salary at the time of the survey was US$70.
2. We use this level of aggregation for analytic reasons. We cannot forget that data must be more disaggregated for targeting, as otherwise too high a proportion of the district's population would be classified into a single category – in other words, one could not detect 'the poorest of the poor'.
3. A new version of the information system was implemented in 1995, based on the software Mapinfo 3.1. for Windows. This software required more powerful hardware (eight megabytes RAM and 40 megabytes hard disk). An ink-jet, colour printer was also purchased. However, due to the continuously decreasing price of computer equipment, the cost of the new system was no different from that of the previous one.

Technical Appendix C
Data Use

PROCEDURES FOR DATA ANALYSIS

The First Step: The General Analysis at the HCRA Level

The first step of the exercise was the analysis of the geographic distribution of the selected socio-economic and environmental variables between the different HCRAs of the district. This was made by means of thematic maps, such as that displayed in map C.1, which refers to the situation of sanitation.

Five HCRAs scored three for both water and sanitation, and four HCRAs scored four for income (we remember that score four indicates a situation of maximum risk, and score one of minimum risk). When these results were combined, the HCRAs of Dom Avelar, Cana Brava, Jardim Nova Esperança and Nova Brasília were detected as the most critical according to socio-economic and environmental criteria.

Subsequently, the spatial distribution of environmental and socio-economic data was compared to the spatial distribution of health data. Data on diarrhoeal diseases were plotted on the map (map C.2).

It was possible to see that diseases were concentrated in the HCRAs of Nova Brasília and Cana Brava, whilst smaller concentrations could be found in Dom Avelar, in the south of Jardim Nova Esperança, and in the centre of Pau da Lima. Even such an overall view tended to confirm to some extent the socio-economic and environmental picture which had emerged previously.

In addition, these data had to be related to the number of residents of each HCRA. They were then analysed in the data bases. The resulting figures are displayed in Table C.1.

MAP C.1

SITUATION OF SANITATION AT THE HCRA LEVEL

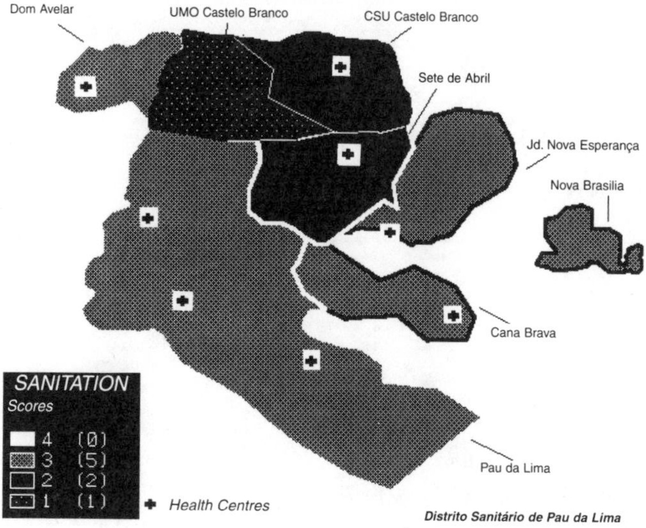

MAP C.2

GEOGRAPHIC DISTRIBUTION OF DIARRHOEAL DISEASES AT THE HCRA LEVEL

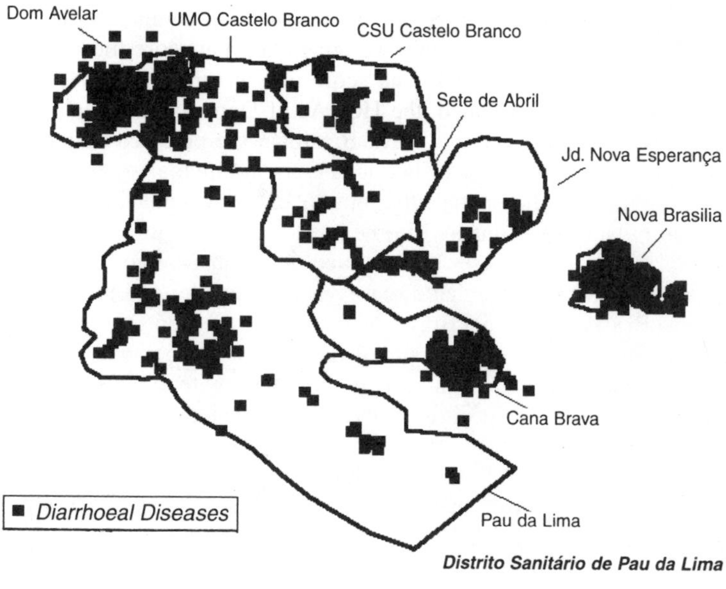

TABLE C.1

DIARRHOEAL DISEASES, 1991, ABSOLUTE NUMBER OF CASES AND INCIDENCE (CASES PER 100,000 INHABITANTS) FOR EACH HCRA

HCRA	N° OF CASES	INCIDENCE
Pau da Lima	68	90.8
Castelo Branco	54	191.4
Dom Avelar	28	285.5
Nova Brasília	109	1327.5
Cana Brava	78	1646.6
Sete de Abril	35	246.4
Jardim Nova Esperança	18	209.8
HEALTH DISTRICT	390	262.4

(*Source*: health district of Pau da Lima)

From Table C.1 we could see that only two out of four HCRAs which had been classified as the most disadvantaged according to socio-economic and environmental criteria appeared also to be the most disadvantaged according to health data (Nova Brasília and Cana Brava).

However, with these data alone we could not know if health indicators actually reflected the different living conditions in each HCRA, or if they were due, instead, to different rates of access to the health services in each HCRA. Possible biases in this respect had to be controlled. Consequently, the data on the population who had registered in the health centres were also analysed. The results are displayed in Table C.2.

TABLE C.2

REGISTERED POPULATION IN THE HEALTH CENTRES, ABSOLUTE NUMBERS AND AS A PERCENTAGE OF THE WHOLE RESIDENT POPULATION OF EACH HCRA

HCRA	REGISTERED PEOPLE	% OF RESIDENT POPULATION
Pau da Lima	5,134	6.9
Castelo Branco	5,569	32.6
Dom Avelar	498	5.6
Nova Brasília	547	3.6
Cana Brava	178	3.8
Sete de Abril	4,136	31.2
Jardim Nova Esperança	726	9.4
TOTAL/AVERAGE FOR THE HEALTH DISTRICT	16,788	11.3

(*Source*: health district of Pau da Lima)

The analysis of Table C.2 indicated that in the majority of the HCRAs the access to health care services was quite limited. The available health data referred to a small percentage of the resident population, especially in the HCRAs previously indicated as the most at risk (Cana Brava and Nova Brasília). It was likely that, in these areas, the same socio-economic factors were responsible for both the high risk of contracting diseases and the low rate of access to the health care services. Nevertheless, it was still impossible to know if such a low access rate was homogeneously distributed within the HCRAs and, if this was not the case, where it was concentrated.

Subsequently the geographic distribution of socio-economic, environmental and health data, as well as of data on access, was analysed at the level of the micro-areas.

The Second Step: The Specific Analysis at the Micro-Area Level

As in the previous analytical step, thematic maps for three socio-economic and environmental variables (sanitation, water and income) were displayed. An example is provided in map C.3 for sanitation.

MAP C.3
SITUATION OF SANITATION AT THE MICRO-AREA LEVEL

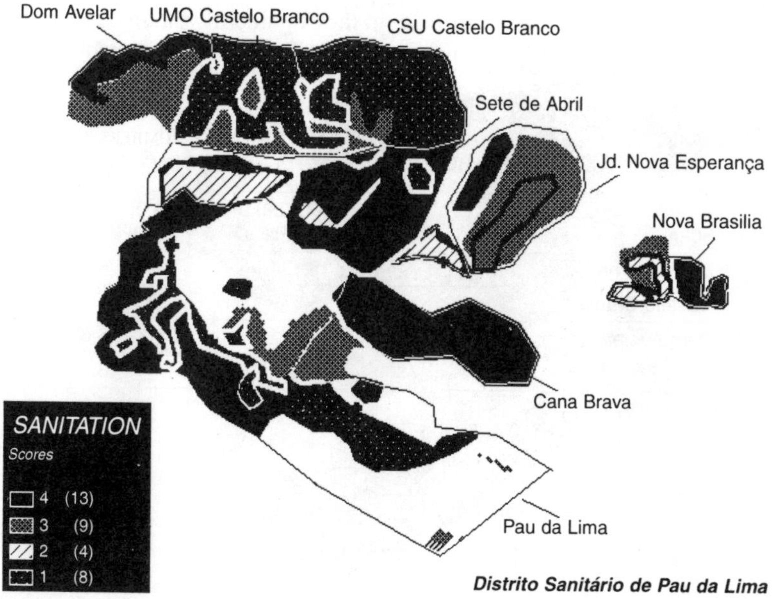

The picture which appeared was very different from the previous one. Eleven micro-areas with the highest score (score four) appeared for water, 13 for sanitation, and five for income. We remember that previously no HCRA had scored four either for water or sanitation.

As suggested by the epidemiologists who were participating in the exercise of data analysis, it was decided to assign different values to the different risk factors. The value four was given to water (the usual determinant of the transmission of diarrhoeal diseases), the value two to sanitation (the lack of which is responsible for the contamination of water), and the value one to income.[1] These values were multiplied by the scores of the variables of each micro-area – but only the scores four and three were considered.

In this way, 29 micro-areas were considered. The resulting values were summed up for each micro-area, and the micro-areas were ranked in a descending order – from the highest resulting value (28) to the lowest (11). This rank was divided into quartiles, and only the first two quartiles – the first 14 micro-areas – were selected as possible targets.

The micro-areas in the first quartile were considered as at high risk (8,637 inhabitants – 5.82 per cent of the district's population); those in the second quartile as at moderate risk (33,176 – 22.33 per cent). These micro-areas are displayed in map C.4.

MAP C.4
MICRO-AREAS AT HIGH RISK AND MODERATE RISK

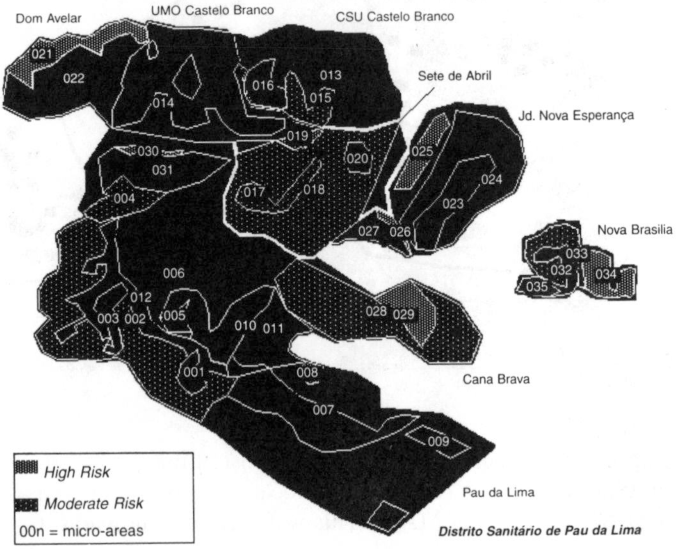

We proceeded, then, to the analysis of health data, by zooming in with the GIS onto each HCRA, and plotting both data on diarrhoeal diseases and data on access to the health care services. Each HCRA with its internal micro-areas was so analysed.

An example of these procedures is shown in maps C.5–C.9, referring respectively to the HCRAs of Nova Brasília and Jardim Nova Esperança.

One micro-area at high risk (MA34, 3,272 inhabitants) and one micro-area at moderate risk (MA33, 1,346 inhabitants) were present in Nova Brasília. In both the micro-areas several cases of diarrhoeal diseases were detected, as shown in map C.5. Most cases were concentrated in the micro-area at high risk (MA34), but diseases were also present in the micro-area at moderate risk (MA33).

MAP C.5

NOVA BRASÍLIA – GEOGRAPHIC DISTRIBUTION OF DIARRHOEAL DISEASES

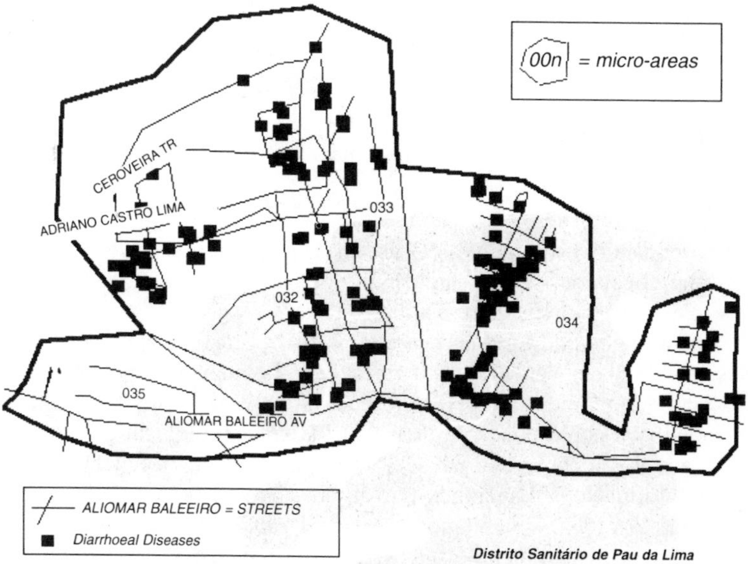

By zooming in the map, we could see that most of the events detected in the micro-area not at risk (MA32) were located on its border – this could be due to the influence of MA33. This was displayed in map C.6.

MAP C.6
NOVA BRASÍLIA – ZOOMING IN THE MICRO-AREA 032

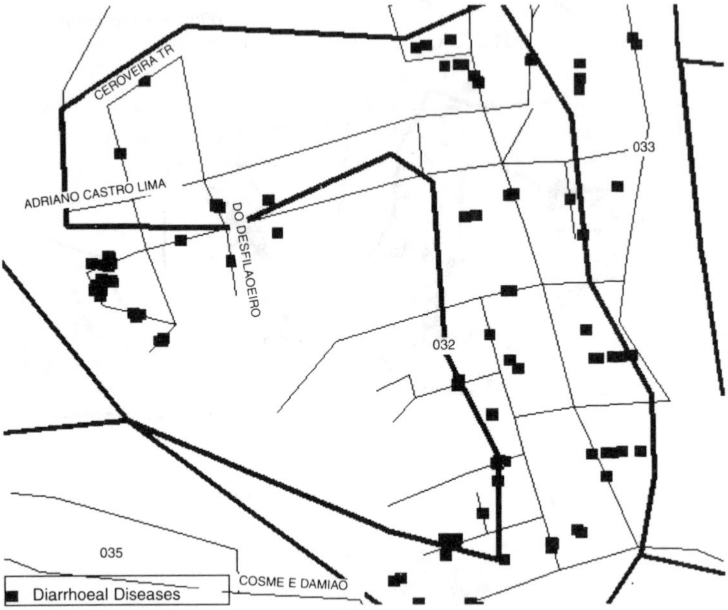

We could see that the pattern of access to the health services was also quite homogeneous – with the possible exception of MA35, in which less registered patients were displayed (map C.7).

According to our previous analysis, in Nova Brasília the rate of access was low (3.6 per cent), but as access was homogeneously distributed among different micro-areas, the presence of biases in health data could be excluded. We could conclude then that the epidemiological picture was valid, and that it confirmed the socio-economic and environmental one.

In Jardim Nova Esperança two micro-areas at high risk had been detected (MA25, 1,418 inhabitants, and MA26, 600 inhabitants). From map C.8 we saw that no reported cases of diarrhoeal diseases were found in the micro-areas at high risk. These were present, instead, in the other micro-areas nearby, and were quite concentrated in MA27.

However, registered patients were absent in both the micro-areas at risk, but were present in the other micro-areas nearby, with a higher concentration precisely in MA27 (map C.9).

MAP C.7

NOVA BRASÍLIA – GEOGRAPHIC DISTRIBUTION OF ACCESS TO THE HEALTH FACILITIES

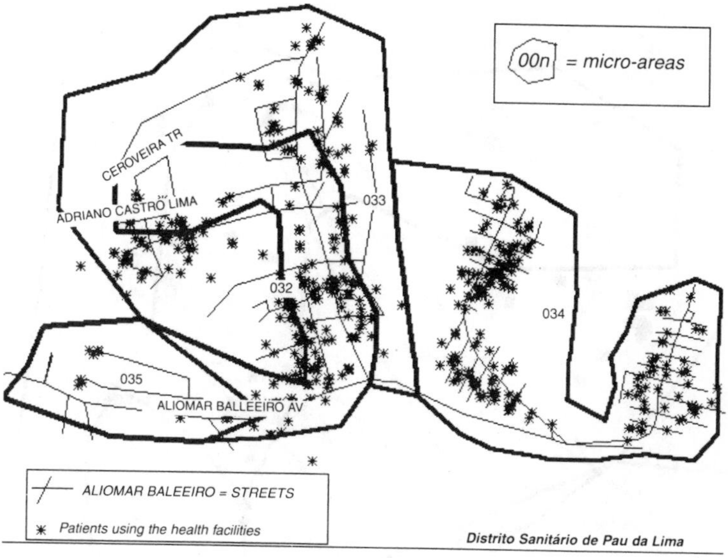

MAP C.8

JARDIM NOVA ESPERANÇA – GEOGRAPHIC DISTRIBUTION OF DIARRHOEAL DISEASES

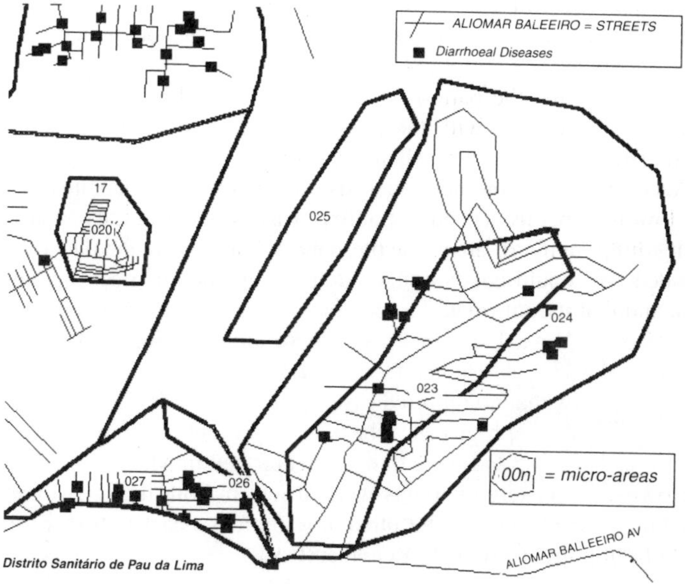

MAP C.9

JARDIM NOVA ESPERANÇA – GEOGRAPHIC DISTRIBUTION OF ACCESS TO THE HEALTH FACILITIES

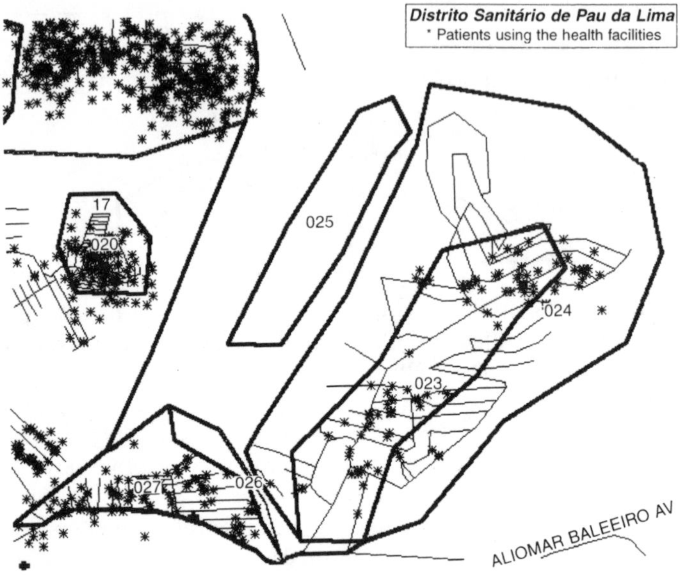

This suggested that the apparent distribution of diseases among the micro-areas could be influenced by the different access pattern. Therefore, the existence of risks on the basis of socio-economic and environmental data could not either be confirmed or rejected by health data.

Targeting

Those micro-areas which showed poor socio-economic and environmental indicators, together with a high concentration of diarrhoeal diseases and a homogeneous access to the health care services, were selected as targets. In this way, the following five micro-areas were selected:

MA34 (Nova Brasília)
MA33 (Nova Brasília)
MA29 (Cana Brava)
MA28 (Cana Brava)
MA18 (Sete de Abril)

These micro-areas had a population of 18,010, representing 12.12 per cent of the population of the health district.

In contrast, eight micro-areas showed poor socio-economic and environmental indicators, together with little or no diseases, and a scarce or absent access to health care services. These were the following micro-areas:

MA25 (Jardim Nova Esperança)
MA26 (Jardim Nova Esperança)
MA8 (Pau da Lima)
MA4 (Pau da Lima)
MA30 (UMO Castelo Branco)
MA15 (CSU Castelo Branco)
MA21 (Dom Avelar)
MA19 (Sete de Abril)

For these micro-areas it was impossible to assess immediately the reliability of health data. Two empirical criteria were set then for selecting further micro-areas at risk.

First, it was established that when medium-to-large micro-areas at risk showed a low occurrence of diseases together with poor access to the health services, but the other micro-areas nearby showed higher occurrence of diseases together with higher access, then health data for the former micro-areas were likely to be biased. A further condition was that the aggregated access rate for the HCRA as a whole was low – this could be due, in fact, to the exclusion of the (relatively large) proportion of population resident in the micro-area at risk. Three micro-areas were selected in this way (MA 25, 26, 21).

Second, biases in health data could also occur when small micro-areas at risk were masked – because of their dimension and the scarce access to health services of their population – within large HCRAs, even if these did not show a high occurrence of diseases. Two more micro-areas were so selected (MA8, MA30).

Finally, both the conditions previously analysed occurred in Sete de Abril, where we found a small micro-area at high risk (MA19) which showed no occurrence of diarrhoeal diseases, together with a medium-to-low access, close to a larger micro-area with a higher access and a higher occurrence of diseases. Consequently, MA19 was selected as a target.

In conclusion, the following eleven micro-areas were selected for targeting:

MA34 (Nova Brasília)
MA33 (Nova Brasília)
MA29 (Cana Brava)
MA28 (Cana Brava)

MA18 (Sete de Abril)
MA25 (Jardim Nova Esperança)
MA26 (Jardim Nova Esperança)
MA8 (Pau da Lima)
MA30 (UMO Castelo Branco)
MA21 (Dom Avelar)
MA19 (Sete de Abril).

These micro-areas are displayed in map C.10.

MAP C.10
MICRO-AREAS SELECTED FOR TARGETING

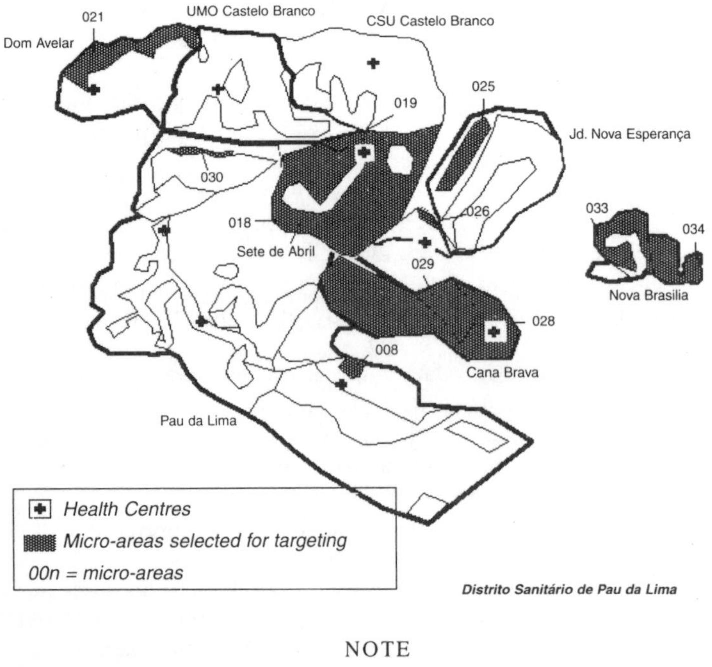

NOTE

1. Such procedures always raise questions, as they are relatively arbitrary, but give results that look very precise. Similar questions could be raised for the attribution of scores in the micro-areas tables. We are arguing, however, that this precision is necessary to simplify data analysis and produce impact on decision-making. Conversely, these arbitrary procedures can be relatively controlled by both systematic rules (as in the attribution of scores) and technical expertise (as in the definition of different values for different risk factors).

References

ABRASCO, *A Experiência SUDS e os Desafios Atuais da Reforma Sanitária* (Rio de Janeiro: ABRASCO, 1989).

Aga Khan Foundation, *Management Information Systems and Microcomputers in Primary Health Care* (Lisbon: report of an international workshop, Nov. 1987).

Automated Methods, *ReGIS/ReGEO User's Guide* (Republic of South Africa: Automated Methods Pty Ltd., 1995).

D. Bennett, 'Explanation in Medical Geography: Evidence and Epistemology', *Social Science and Medicine*, 33, 4 (1991), pp. 339–46.

P. Blunt, 'Strategies for Enhancing Organisational Effectiveness in the Third World', *Public Administration and Development*, 10 (1990), pp. 299–313.

D.W. Brinkerhoff and M.D. Ingle, 'Integrating Blueprint and Process: a Structured Flexibility Approach to Development Management', *Public Administration and Development,* 9 (1989), pp. 487–503.

D.W. Brinkerhoff and R. Klauss, 'Managerial Roles for Social Development Management', *Public Administration and Development*, 5, 2 (1985) pp. 145–56.

J. Brodman, *Microcomputers Adoption in Developing Countries: Old Management Style and New Information Systems* (University of Maryland: International Management Development Center, 1985).

D.J. Casley and D.A. Lury, *Data Collection in Developing Countries* (Oxford: Clarendon Press, 1987).

R. Chambers, 'Rapid Rural Appraisal: Rationale and Repertoire', *Public Administration and Development*, 1 (1981), pp.95–106.

R. Chambers, *Rural Development: Putting the Last First* (London: Longman, 1983).

R. Chambers, *Managing Rural Development: Ideas and Experience from East Africa* (West Hartford, CT: Kumarian Press, 1985).

R. Chambers, 'Bureaucratic Reversals and Local Diversity', *IDS Bulletin,* 19, 4 (1988a), pp. 50–56.

R. Chambers, *Normal Professionalism and the Early Project Process: Problems and Solutions* (University of Sussex, Brighton: IDS Discussion Paper 247, 1988b).

L.C. Chen *et al.*, *Classification of energy-protein malnutrition by anthropometry and subsequent risk of mortality* (Bangladesh: International Centre for Diarrhoeal Disease, mimeo, 1978).

A.H. Chorny, 'El Enfoque Estratégico para el Desarrollo de Recursos Humanos', *Educ Med Salud*, 24, 1 (1990), pp. 27–51.

D. Conyers and P. Hills, *An Introduction to Development Planning in the Third World* (Chichester, New York, Brisbane, Toronto, Singapore: John Wiley and Sons, 1984).

J. Dangermond, 'Geographic Information System Technology and Development Planning', *Regional Development Dialogue,* 11, 3 (1990), pp. 1–14.

C.M. de Almeida, *Os Atalhos da Mudança na Saúde no Brasil. Serviços em Nível Local: Nove Estudos de Caso – Uma Análise Comparativa* (Rio de Janeiro: PAHO/WHO, 1989).

E.C. de Araujo and C.F. Teixeira, *Distritalização do Setor Saúde na Bahia. Momentos, Problemas e Perspectivas* (Salvador, Brazil: paper for the Italo-Brazilian meeting on NHS reform, May 1989).

E. de Kadt, 'Making Health Policy Management Intersectoral: Issues of Information Analysis and Use in Less Developed Countries', *Social Science and Medicine*, 29, 4 (1989), pp. 503–14.

E. de Kadt and R. Tasca, *Promovendo a Equidade: Um Novo Enfoque com Base no Setor Saúde* (São Paulo: Hucitec/Cooperação Italiana em Saúde, 1993). The English version is also available: *Promoting Equity: A New Approach from the Health Sector* (Washington, DC: PAHO, 1993).

M.J.C. de Lepper, H.J. Scholten and R.M. Stern (eds), *The Added Value of Geographical Information Systems in Public and Environmental Health* (Dordrecht, Boston, London: Kluwer Academic Publishers/WHO Regional Office for Europe, 1991).

P. Dickens, *Urban Sociology. Society, Locality and Nature* (Hemel Hempstead, Hertfordshire: Harvester Wheatsheaf, 1990).

Distrito Sanitário Pau da Lima, *Plano Operativo do Distrito Sanitário de Pau da Lima* (Salvador, Brazil: mimeo, 1989).

R. Dore, 'Community Development in the 1970s', in R. Dore and Z. Mars (eds), *Community Development* (London/Paris: Croom Helm/UNESCO, 1981), pp. 13–46.

R. V. Fernandes, *Estudo sobre o perfil sócio-econômico e de saúde do Distrito Sanitário Pau da Lima* (Salvador, Brazil: mimeo, 1989).

N.G. Fielding and R.G. Lee (eds), *Using Computers in Qualitative Research* (London: Sage, 1991).

Gerência Distrito Sanitário Pau da Lima, *Boletim Epidemiológico Janeiro à Junho 1993* (Salvador, Brazil: mimeo, 1991).

G. Gran, *Development by People* (New York: Praeger, 1983).

M.C.L. Guimarães, F. Ripa di Meana, E. Foccoli and C.F. Teixeira, *A Cooperação Italiana no Brasil e o Desenvolvimento Gerencial dos Sistemas Locais de Saúde* (São Paulo: mimeo July 1991).

B. Harris, 'Urban and Regional Planning in the Third World with a Geographic Information System Support', *Regional Development Dialogue,* 11, 3 (1990), pp. 17–62.

R. Heaver, *Bureaucratic Politics and Incentives in the Management of Rural Development* (Washington, DC: World Bank Staff Working Paper 537, 1982).

R. Heaver, *Adapting a Training and Visit Extension System for Family Planning, Health and Nutrition Programs* (Washington, DC: World Bank Staff Working Paper 662, 1984).

A.O. Hirschman, *Development Projects Observed* (Washington, DC: Brookings Institutions, 1967).

M.D. Ingle, *Evaluating the Appropriateness of Microcomputers for Management Applications in Developing Countries* (New York: Development Project Management Center, 1983).

A. Israel, *Institutional Development. Incentives to Performance* (Baltimore: Johns Hopkins University Press, 1987).

M.N. Kiggundu, J.J. Jorgensen and T. Hafsi, 'Administrative Theory and Practice in Developing Countries: A Synthesis', *Administrative Science Quarterly*, 28 (1983), pp. 66–84.

D.C. Korten, 'Community Organisation and Rural Development, a Learning Process Approach', *Public Administration Review,* 40, 5 (1980), pp. 481–511.

D.C. Korten, 'The Management of Social Transformation', *Public Administration Review*, 41 (Nov.–Dec. 1981), pp. 609–18.

D.C. Korten, 'Rural Development Programming: The Learning Process Approach', in D.C. Korten and R. Klauss (eds), *People-centred Development: Contributions Towards Theory and Planning Frameworks* (West Hartford, CT: Kumarian Press, 1984), pp.176–88.

M. Landau and R. Stout Jr, 'To Manage Is Not To Control: Or the Folly of Type II Errors', *Public Administration Review*, 39, 2 (March/April 1979), pp. 148–56.

H. Leibenstein, *Beyond Economic Man: a New Foundation for Micro-economics* (Cambridge, MA: Harvard University Press, 1976).

D.K. Leonard, *Workshops on Organisational Analysis* (University of Sussex, Brighton: notes for the IDS Seminars, June 1991).

C.E. Lindblom, 'The Science of Muddling Through', *Public Administration Review*, 29 (1959), pp. 79–99.

C.E. Lindblom, 'The Sociology of Planning: Thought and Social Interaction', in M. Bornstein (ed.), *Economic Planning East and West* (Cambridge MA: Ballinger Publishing Company, 1975), pp. 23–60.

M. Lipton and S. Maxwell, *The New Poverty Agenda: An Overview* (University of Sussex, Brighton: Institute of Development Studies Discussion Papers 306, 1992).

L. Lomnitz Adler, *Networks and Marginality. Life in a Mexican Shantytown* (New York, San Francisco and London: Academic Press, 1982).

R. Longhurst (ed.), 'Rapid Rural Appraisal', *Bulletin of the Institute of Development Studies*, 12, 4 (1981).

S. Madon, 'Introducing Administrative Reform through the Application of Computer-based Information Systems: a Case-study from India', *Public Administration and Development*, 13 (1993), pp. 37–48.

L. Manderson and P. Aaby, 'An Epidemic in the Field? Rapid Assessment Procedures and Health Research', *Social Science and Medicine*, 35, 7 (1992) pp. 839–50.

J.D. Mayer, 'Challenges to Understanding Spatial Patterns of Disease: Philosophical Alternatives to Logical Positivism', *Social Science and Medicine,* 35, 4 (1992), pp. 579–87.

G.J. McCall and J.L. Simmons (eds), *Issues in Participant Observation* (Reading, MA: Addison-Wesley, 1969).

E.V. Mendes, *O Sistema Unificado e Descentralizado de Saúde no Atual Contexto da Reforma Sanitária Brasileira* (Natal, Brazil: mimeo, 1987).

E.V. Mendes, *Sistemas Locais de Saúde* (Brasília: mimeo, June 1989).

E.V. Mendes, 'Importancia de los Sistemas Locales de Salud en la Transformación de los Sistemas Nacionales de Salud', in J.M. Paganini and R. Capote Mir (eds), *Los Sistemas Locales de Salud: Conceptos, Métodos, Experiencias* (Washington, DC: PAHO, Scientific Publication 519, 1990), pp. 21–7.

E.V. Mendes, C.F. Teixeira, E.C. Araujo and M.R.L. Cardoso, 'Distritos Sanitários: Conceitos-Chave', in E.V. Mendes (ed.), *Distrito Sanitário. O processo social de mudança das práticas sanitárias no Sistema Único de Saúde* (São Paulo e Rio de Janeiro: Hucitec/Abrasco, 1993), pp. 159–85.

J. Moris, *Managing Induced Rural Development* (Bloomington, IN: International Development Institute, 1981).

J. Moris, *What Organisation Theory Has to Offer Third World Agricultural Managers* (London: ODI, undated).

F. Notarbartolo di Villarosa, *A Estimativa Rápida e a Divisão do Território no Distrito Sanitário. Manual de Instruçôes* (Brasília: PAHO, Brazilian Office, Série Desenvolvimento de Serviços de Saúde N°11, 1993).

F. Notarbartolo di Villarosa, R. Tasca and R.V. Fernandes, 'Análise da Situação Sócio-sanitária, Microlocalização e Participação no Distrito Sanitário de Pau da Lima', *Revista Baiana de Saúde Pública*, 17, 1–4 (1990), pp.7–14.

F. Notarbartolo di Villarosa and A. Bunschaft, *A estruturação dos bairros da Região Urbana de Pau da Lima* (Salvador, Brazil: mimeo, 1990).

F. Notarbartolo di Villarosa and A. Bunschaft, 'Bambini di Strada e Accesso ai Servizi Socio-sanitari a Salvador de Bahia, Brasile', *Percorsi di Integrazione,* 2, 1 (1993), pp. 23–30.

R.E. Pahl, 'The Restructuring of Capital, the Local Political Economy and Household Work Strategies', in D. Gregory and J. Urry (eds), *Social Relations and Spatial Structures* (London: Macmillan, 1984), pp. 243–64.

PAHO, *Documento CD 33/14, Resolución XV–XXXIII del Comité Directivo* (Washington: PAHO, 1988).

PAHO, *Administración Estratégica Local. Una propuesta para la discusión (versión preliminar)* (Washington, DC: PAHO, 1991).

S. Paul, 'The Strategic Management of Development Programmes: Evidence from an International Study', *International Review of Administrative Sciences*, 49, 1 (1983a), pp. 73–86.

S. Paul, *Strategic Management of Development Programmes: Guidelines for Action* (Geneva: ILO, Management Development Series N° 19, 1983b).

S. Paul, *Institutional Development in World Bank Projects: a Cross-Sectoral Review* (Washington, DC: World Bank, Policy, Research and External Affairs Working Papers, WP 392, 1990).

F. Pedrão, *Urbanização, Informalidade e Saúde em Salvador* (Salvador, Brazil: mimeo, 1990).

S.B. Peterson, *From Processing to Analyzing: Intensifying the Use of Microcomputers in Development Bureaucracies* (Cambridge, MA: Harvard Institute for International Development, Development Discussion Paper, 1990a).

S.B. Peterson, 'Institutionalizing Microcomputers in Developing Bureaucracies: Theory and Practice from Kenya', *Information Technology for Development*, 5, 3 (1990b), pp. 277–325.

C. Pinto, 'Injusto e Perverso', *Folha de São Paulo* (3 March 1996), p. 19.

M. Reed, *Redirections in Organizational Analysis* (London: Tavistock, 1985).

R. Rego, E. de Souza, R. Tasca and R.V. Fernandes, *Morbidade na demanda às unidades da rede básica no Distrito Sanitário de Pau da Lima* (Salvador, Brazil: mimeo, 1989).

D.A. Rondinelli, 'The Dilemma of Development Administration: Complexity and Uncertainty in Control-Oriented Bureaucracies', *World Politics,* 35, 1 (1982), pp. 43–72.

D.A. Rondinelli, *Development Projects as Policy Experiments* (London: Methuen, 1983).

G. Rose, *Deciphering Sociological Research* (London: Macmillan, 1982).

SESAB, *Elementos para o Desenho da Estratégia de Implantação dos Distritos Sanitários* (Salvador, Brazil: mimeo, July 1988).

W.J. Siffin, 'Two Decades of Public Administration in Developing Countries', in L.D. Stifel, J.E. Black and J.S. Coleman (eds), *Education and Training for Public Sector Management in Developing Countries* (New York: The Rockfeller Foundation, Working Papers, 1977).

F. Stewart, *Protecting the Poor during Adjustment in Latin America and the Caribbean in the 1980s. How Adequate was the World Bank Response?* (Turin/Oxford: Centro Studi Luca d'Agliano/Queen Elizabeth House Development Studies Working Papers 44, 1992).

C.F. Sweet and P. Wiesel, 'Process vs. Blueprint Models for Designing Rural Development Projects', in G. Honadle and R. Klauss (eds.), *International Development Administration. Implementation Analysis for Development Projects* (New York: Praeger Special Studies, 1979), pp. 127–45.

J.D. Thompson, *Organisations in Action* (New York: Mc Graw-Hill, 1967).

UNDP, *Human Development Report 1990* (Oxford: Oxford University Press, 1990).

N. Uphoff, 'Participatory Evaluation of Farmer Organizations' Capacity for

Development Tasks', *Agricultural Administration and Extension*, 30 (1988), pp. 43–64.

E. Veronesi, *Relazione sulla missione presso la Segreteria della Sanità dello Stato di Bahia* (Rome: mimeo, 1989).

World Bank, *World Development Report 1990* (Washington, DC: World Bank, 1990).

J.S. Wunsch, 'Sustaining Third World Infrastructure Investments: Decentralization and Alternative Strategies', *Public Administration and Development,* 11 (1991), pp. 5–23.

Index

Index